D0821290

PUT TO WORK

PUT TO WORK

Relief Programs in the Great Depression

NANCY E. ROSE

CORNERSTONE ·B·O·O·K·S·

**MONTHLY REVIEW PRESS
NEW YORK**

Library of Congress Cataloging-in-Publication Data
Rose, Nancy Ellen.
   Put to work : relief programs in the Great Depression / by Nancy E. Rose.
      p. cm. — (Cornerstone books)
   ISBN 0-85345-871-5 : $10.00
   1. Public service employment—United States—History. 2. Depressions—1929—
United States. 3. Public works—United States—Employees—History. 4. Full em-
ployment policies—United States—History. 5. Job creation—United
States—History. 6. Public service employment—United States. 7. Full employ-
ment policies—United States. 8. Welfare recipients—Employment—United
States. I. Title. II. Series: Cornerstone books (New York, N.Y.)
HD5713.6.U54R67   1993
331.13'77'0973—   dc20   93-26617
                                                                              CIP

Monthly Review Press
122 West 27th Street
New York, NY 10001

Manufactured in the United States of America
10 9 8 7 6 5 4 3 2 1

For Jesse and Zachary

CONTENTS

ACKNOWLEDGMENTS

In a sense this book has been in process for the past fifteen years, from the time when I was a graduate student at the University of Massachusetts and my investigation into the origins of the U.S. welfare system led me to the 1930s relief programs. At that time, discussions with Sam Bowles were particularly important in helping me define the issues and develop a theoretical framework.

Paul Sweezy's encouragement when I first met him in 1987 was critical to my extending the early work into a book. His enthusiasm and insistence about the importance of a book on the Works Progress Administration (WPA) and the other Depression-era work programs was contagious. The editorial work of Susan Lowes, Director of Monthly Review Press, was essential to the book's process, sometimes making it feel like a collaborative venture. Her careful editing, as well as questions and comments, kept me focussed on describing the programs in a way that would bring them to life. Beth Stroud searched through the National

Archives in Washington, D.C., as well as other sources, for the many evocative pictures of the New Deal programs. And grants from the National Endowment for the Humanities and California State University, San Bernardino, allowed me to spend several weeks at the National Archives examining materials collected as part of the programs.

My family and friends have been supportive and encouraging. My sister Jill, brother Andy, and mother and father have been anxiously awaiting the book's publication. My children, Jesse and Zachary, have been patient when I wanted to write. Comments on some of the chapters from Kathi West and Mayo Toruño were very helpful. And special thanks go to Carol Stack for suggesting the title of the book years ago when I first told her about this project.

Ever since I discovered the 1930s work programs, I have taken delight in finding projects built under their auspices. Even my hometown of Crestline, California, has one: Lake Gregory, which is the focal point of the town and is used for a variety of recreational activities, was created by a dam built as part of the WPA. Yet I am struck by the fact that although people are often aware of the WPA, few have heard of the even more innovative programs that preceded it—the Federal Emergency Relief Administration (FERA) and the Civil Works Administration (CWA). Since these two programs have been the focus of much of my research, I have often felt that I am rescuing them from the dustbin of history. Hopefully, the creativity and respect for individuals that characterized all of the 1930s relief programs can provide an alternative to the constricted visions and punitive policies that have dominated government work program discussions and procedures in the 1980s and 1990s.

INTRODUCTION

Continuing high unemployment and the personal and societal distress it brings in its wake has fueled ongoing debate about the welfare system. While conservatives advocate mean-spirited and punitive policies, liberals focus on education and training programs. Both conservatives and liberals generally agree on the need for mandatory work programs: that welfare recipients should be forced to work at some job (other than taking care of their children) in order to prove they deserve aid.

The 1930s was also a time of economic distress, with millions of people out of work. But instead of mandatory work programs that humiliate and stigmatize the poor, the Roosevelt administration's New Deal developed massive government job-creation programs. These are often remembered as inefficient and unnecessary "make-work," or "boondoggles," as they were called at the time. However, a closer examination reveals that these often accurate criticisms followed almost inevitably from the constraints imposed on the programs. Furthermore, if the criteria of people's needs is used in place of the logic of business profits, these programs can be seen as a real success.

Although the Works Progress Administration (WPA), is the best-known of the 1930s work programs, it was preceded by two programs that were even more interesting and controversial. The Federal Emergency Relief Administration (FERA), from May 1933 through December 1935, briefly interrupted by the massive Civil Works Administration (CWA) during the winter of 1933-1934, came under intense attack from the business sector. Along with complaints that the programs were boondoggles, charges that payments were too high and that some projects competed unfairly with private enterprise were frequent. The policy vacuum created by years of Hoover administration inaction and the maelstrom of criticism that swirled around the programs sometimes led federal relief officials to change policies in midstream in response to these objections.

By the time the WPA began in September 1935, the most contentious issues had been settled. Although there was a great deal of criticism of the WPA, it nevertheless lasted into the 1940s, and was only phased out as mobilization for World War II increased jobs and finally brought the economy out of the depression.

The FERA, CWA, and WPA were a far cry from current government work programs. Instead of the contemporary focus on mandatory programs designed to punish welfare recipients, these were voluntary programs that routinely provided work each month for between 1.4 and 3.3 million people—and for 4.4 million at the height of the CWA. (In contrast, the largest voluntary work program since then was CETA's Public Service Employment program, which provided work for only 742,000 people at its height in March 1978.) Payments were based on private-sector wage rates. And a huge variety of socially useful work was done. Across the country, public buildings were constructed and renovated, recreational facilities were built, roads were made and repaired, classes were taught, surveys were con-

A girl trying on a dress made in a WPA sewing project and distributed in a school. [National Archives]

ducted, plays and musical performances were staged, murals were painted, garments and household goods were produced for relief families, and school lunches were served to needy children.

While there is much to applaud in these programs, there were limitations. Although millions of people were put to work, millions more never got on the rolls. Furthermore, the programs were designed primarily for white male heads of household: women and people of color were marginalized. As we will see in what follows, they had a more difficult time establishing eligibility and obtaining placements, and they also received lower average wages compared to white men.

Having a clearer picture of the 1930s work programs can help support arguments for the return of similar programs today—

this time in a way that would focus on women and people of color as well as white men. It is particularly important to understand how the barrage of criticism by the business sector constrained the size of the programs, the level of payments, and the types of projects, especially those in which consumer goods were produced. In fact, it was these constraints, especially the prohibition against competition with the private sector and the requirement that a maximum of labor and a minimum of machinery be used, that led almost inevitably to charges of make-work, inefficiency, and "boondoggles."

We turn now to this story.

1

THE GREAT DEPRESSION AND THE BEGINNINGS OF THE NEW DEAL

Picture the 1920s, the "Roaring Twenties": flappers, speakeasies, parties, and bathtub gin provide the background for the memories of gaiety and prosperity that characterized the years immediately following World War I. Automobiles were a catalyst for growth, as people could live further from their workplaces, and whole new industries sprang up to supply and service cars. Yet most working people missed out on the good times. Between 1920 and 1929, the income of the bottom 93 percent of the population rose only 6 percent, while that of the top 7 percent increased almost 200 percent. By 1929, when the stock market crashed, more than two of every five families were poor.[1]

Now picture the 1930s. The euphoria of the 1920s has given way to mass poverty and protest. Factories are operating below

An apple seller at work in front of his Hooverville home in New York City in 1931. [Culver Pictures, Inc.]

capacity or have closed entirely, while unemployment has soared, until by 1933 it is a huge 25 percent of the entire labor force—and a full 37 percent of the industrial labor force.[2] And neither figure includes "discouraged" workers, those who have given up looking for jobs. The unemployed are selling apples on streetcorners to make a few pennies or standing in line at soup kitchens, while food is rotting in the fields because the farmers cannot sell it for enough to make it worth harvesting. Houses are boarded up and farms foreclosed as the owners fail to meet their mortgage payments, and apartments are vacant since people have no money for rent. The growing numbers of homeless are building ramshackle temporary housing out of cardboard and wood on the outskirts of cities across the country. Panicked depositors are withdrawing their money from the banks, which are failing one after the other, while barter is replacing cash transactions. Rising unemployment and falling incomes are leading to declining tax revenues, and in many towns teachers are out of work and children are out of school.

Herbert Hoover, who was president in 1929 when the Depression began, approached the growing crisis by following conventional economic wisdom: the market should be left to function "naturally" until the economy "bottomed out" and wages and prices again began to rise. But by March 1933, when Franklin Roosevelt became president, the bottom still seemed nowhere in sight. Since 1929 production had fallen by one-third, prices and wages by one-quarter, and investment in new plant and equipment was at a virtual standstill. Growing unemployment was forcing down hours as well as wages, so that even those who still had jobs had less to spend.[3]

RELIEF BEFORE THE GREAT DEPRESSION

Before the Depression, relief came from two main sources: private charities and local governments. Government relief was restricted and punitive. It was only available to town residents; nonresidents, called "transients," did not qualify. Establishing residency was often a complicated task, as people had to live in a town for between one and five years (depending on the town) and prove that they could become self-supporting. Relief was based on a "means-test," in which an applicant had to show that all other sources of aid, including from relatives, had been exhausted. And the amount of aid was low and usually limited to "in-kind" food, clothing, fuel, and medical care.

A distinction was made between the "deserving poor," who received relief while continuing to live in their communities, and the "undeserving poor," who were forced into workhouses, poorhouses, or poor farms, where they were required to work for their aid. The "deserving" poor were generally white, female, U.S.-

born widows, while the "undeserving poor" included almost everyone else: able-bodied men, people of color, recent immigrants, and women who had had children out of wedlock or had been deserted by their husbands. In order to receive relief, these men and women were often required to perform work that was clearly useless—digging ditches and filling them up again, or moving piles of stones from one side of a workyard to the other and back—but which the overseers of the poor believed would discourage anyone who could possibly work for wages from going on relief.

Only when the severe recessions that had occurred periodically since the 1830s sent unemployment high enough to raise concern about widespread and prolonged joblessness among white, U.S.-born male heads of household did local governments develop less stigmatizing work projects. Most of these were for white men and they primarily involved public works, such as constructing and repairing roads and public facilities. Other projects included chopping wood in woodyards and such maintenance work as collecting garbage and shoveling snow. Some cities established sewing rooms for women, who were generally paid less than men, as well as for men who were not able to labor outdoors. These programs were usually expanded in the winter, when the need for food and shelter increased.

In addition, some U.S.-born white widows received direct relief from Mothers' Pensions or Mothers' Aid. First enacted in 1911 in Missouri and Illinois, by 1921 this program had been adopted in one form or another in forty states. Under all of these programs, African-Americans and other people of color received little or nothing.

PROTEST AND SURVIVAL

As the Depression deepened and destitution increased in the early 1930s, a "fathomless pessimism" spread across the country.[4] Suicides were common, especially among middle-class men who

Table 1
Number of Unemployed, 1929–1943*

Year	Number	Percent
1929	1,550,000	3.2
1930	4,340,000	8.9
1931	8,020,000	16.3
1932	12,060,000	24.1
1933	12,830,000	25.2
1934	11,340,000	22.0
1935	10,610,000	20.3
1936	9,030,000	17.0
1937	7,700,000	14.3
1938	10,390,000	19.1
1939	9,480,000	17.2
1940	8,120,000	14.6
1941	5,560,000	9.9
1942	2,660,000	4.7
1943	1,070,000	1.9

*References for figures and tables will be found on p. 138.

could no longer support their families. Transiency increased as people left their home communities in search of jobs, or simply a better life, elsewhere. Estimates of homeless transients varied widely, and figures ranging from 500,000 to 5 million were cited in the press. The Depression transients were not only men: single women and families swelled their ranks. People slept in cars and in parks, while some went to jail to get a night's sleep and some food. And many took to the road or lived for a while in one of the communities of improvised housing—called Hoovervilles—that grew up around the country.[5]

Some of the unemployed developed innovative, and often illegal, ways of surviving. Unemployed miners in western Pennsylvania dug narrow and dangerous shafts on company property in order to bootleg coal—an "industry" that by 1933 provided work for between 15,000 and 20,000 people and was applauded by local businesspeople, politicians, and even the police because it kept the local economy from total collapse.

The depression in farming had begun earlier, in 1926, when prices of agricultural commodities started to fall. By the early 1930s prices were so low that the wages paid to workers for harvesting crops were often greater than the amount the farmers would receive from their sale. In response, elaborate systems of barter were developed through what were called "self-help cooperatives," as unemployed workers traded hours of farm work in return for food crops that would otherwise have rotted in the field. These cooperatives, which started in Seattle in the summer of 1931, spread throughout the country but were most successful in southern California, where the mild climate made year-round farming possible.[6]

Hog and dairy farmers in the Midwest, hard hit by the Depression, formed the Farm Holiday Association. They organized "holidays," or strikes, to demand prices equal to the "cost of production" for their goods, and dumped milk on the highways to dramatize their actions. They also turned farm foreclosures into penny auctions, roaming the crowds with shotguns to ensure that no one bid more than a few cents for the animals and implements that were up for auction—and then returned them to the original owners. In some areas the "penny auctions" were so successful that bankers called a halt to foreclosures.[7]

Starting in early 1930, unemployed councils, organized by the Communist Party, began to lead hunger marches to demand more relief. On March 6, 1932, which was proclaimed International Unemployment Day, hunger marches took place throughout the country. In cities where Unemployed Councils were strong enough, notably New York and Chicago, they organized "rent riots," forcing landlords to return the evicted and their belongings to their homes, and to reconnect gas and electricity

Striking milk producers dumping milk on the Rochester-Syracuse highway. [AP/Wide World Photos]

lines when they had been turned off. In general, cities with strong Unemployed Councils generally provided better relief.[8]

Demonstrations and protests intensified. "Food riots" and "hunger riots" became more common as crowds of people stormed stores and took the food they needed. Many storeowners did not call the police for fear of publicity, which they believed would lead the idea to spread even further.[9]

Police violence against the demonstrators also increased. In March 1932, police attacked a hunger march at a Ford Motor Company plant in Michigan, killing three marchers and injuring fifty more. The most often cited instance of police violence during the early 1930s, and one that provoked a strong outcry when it happened, involved the Bonus Expeditionary Force, or Bonus

Army, of World War I veterans who went to Washington, D.C., in June 1932 to demand early payment of their veterans' bonus. Although the measure was defeated, veterans and their families continued to pour into the nation's capital. By the end of July approximately 20,000 people had gathered there, setting up a Hooverville not far from the capitol building. The presence of women and children did not deter the federal government from sending cavalry, infantry, and tanks under the command of General Douglas MacArthur to set fire to the encampment and rout them out.[10]

The massive use of force against a ragtag group that included women and children was the result of a growing fear that some of the population was close to revolt. Farmers were pouring milk on the highways, women and men were looting stores, thousands were marching to demand more relief—little wonder that the government was worried. Dixon Wecter reported a study in the early 1930s which found that nearly one-fourth of the unemployed thought that "a revolution might be a very good thing for this country."[11] And conservative Congressman Hamilton Fish summed up the anxiety among the upper echelon of society when he told the House of Representatives that "if we don't give [security] under the existing system, the people will change the system. Make no mistake about that."[12]

HOOVER OFFERS LITTLE HELP

As the Depression worsened in the early 1930s, the need for relief quickly surpassed the available funds from both private charities and the government. A 1932 survey conducted by the American Association of Social Workers found that only 25 percent of the unemployed were receiving any relief at all. And although many cities, especially the large industrial ones, had increased relief expenditures and set up public works projects, falling tax revenues were making this increasingly difficult.[13]

Escalating protest led local officials to ask for state and federal

A Bonus Army rally in Washington, D.C., in 1932. A huge Hoover-ville can be seen in the background. [Culver Pictures, Inc.]

aid. In Chicago, where half of the labor force was unemployed and Socialists and Communists were organizing mass demonstrations, the mayor begged for $150 million in immediate relief. He argued that this would be far better than sending in federal troops to quell the riots he believed would otherwise occur. And New York City demonstrations led by the Communist Party consistently drew thousands of participants.[14]

New York was one of the first states to respond to these pleas for funds. In November 1931, under the leadership of Governor Franklin Roosevelt, the legislature established the Temporary Emergency Relief Administration (TERA) to provide money to cities for unemployment relief. Other states followed suit, and by the end of 1932 twenty-two states were providing some form of relief.[15]

The state governments were also strapped for funds, however. Yet when they turned to the federal government, President Hoover refused to help. Instead he clung resolutely to his belief that the government should stay out of the economy and the federal budget should remain balanced. In fact, although several bills that would have provided federal funds for unemployment relief and public works were introduced into Congress during his term as President. Maintaining that "nobody is actually starving," Hoover vetoed any that passed. He was supported by business groups, including the National Association of Manufacturers and the Chamber of Commerce, whose leaders argued that an unemployment fund would "promote idleness, stifle individual initiative, and impair individual responsibility, and thus materially increase unemployment." This was the business sector's attitude; it would be repeated again and again over the next few years.[16]

Hoover argued further that private charities should provide the needed money. In October 1930, he had established the President's Emergency Committee on Employment, which was supposed to stimulate private donations for relief and encourage private industry to "give a job" and "spread the work." But there were few jobs to give and little work to spread. The committee was replaced in August 1931 by the President's Organization on Unemployment Relief, which also appealed to the public for funds. When it co-sponsored a fundraising drive with the Association of Community Chests and Councils, the publicity was enthusiastic: "America will feel the thrill of a great spiritual experience ... millions of dollars will be raised in cities and towns throughout the land, and the fear of cold and hunger will be banished from the hearts of thousands ..." But there was little response, and in July 1932 Hoover was forced to sign the Emergency Relief and Construction Act, which established a mechanism for providing federal loans—not grants—to the states to use for relief. These funds were allocated very cautiously and only $30 million had been borrowed by the end of 1932. Compared to the billions that would soon be spent on relief, this was a drop in the bucket.[17]

THE NEW DEAL TO THE RESCUE

By the time Franklin Roosevelt took office on March 4, 1933, the economy was almost at a standstill and it was clear that existing relief arrangements were not coming close to meeting the needs of the unemployed. In addition to idle workers and idle factories, there were increasing numbers of idle banks—thirty-eight states had declared "bank holidays," a euphemism for closing the banks' doors. The New York Stock Exchange and the Chicago Board of Trade had closed as well.

The time was ripe for change and the new administration, not constrained by Hoover's conservative economic doctrine, was ready to take on the task. Roosevelt brought to Washington a group of mostly young men—known as the "brain trust"—to develop policy and fashion legislation. In the first one hundred days after his inauguration, his administration proposed, and Congress passed, an array of legislation designed to stop the economic decline and get people back to work. The cumulative effect of all this activity was evident across the country: people felt that something was finally being done to address the crisis. Each program was announced with great fanfare. There were parades in support of some of the new legislation. President Roosevelt made frequent radio addresses, which kept people informed and helped restore their faith in the system. In many homes, pictures of the President were placed in honored positions over the mantelpiece.[18]

Putting the banking system back on a sound footing was the first order of business, and the day after taking office Roosevelt declared a bank holiday for all the remaining banks. Four days later Congress passed the Emergency Banking Act, which allowed banks to reopen only if the government could assure their soundness. Signalling Roosevelt's concurrence with the fiscal orthodoxy of a balanced budget, Congress passed an Economy Act, which cut federal expenditures by $500 million. In fact, the massive amounts of money that were forthcoming for relief were possible only because they were labeled emergency expenditures.

Next came legislation that set up a series of agencies—known as the "alphabet agencies"—to deal with the problems in manufacturing, agriculture, and finance. The Agricultural Adjustment Act set up the Agricultural Adjustment Administration (AAA) to increase agricultural prices by reducing supply, and was passed one day before a strike scheduled by the Farm Holiday Association. The National Industrial Recovery Act (NIRA) established the National Recovery Administration (NRA), which brought together businesspeople and workers under the wing of the government to negotiate prices and wages through "codes of fair competition." It also contained Section 7(a), in which the federal government finally recognized the right of workers to organize unions of their own choosing, and led to a tremendous increase in union activity. The NIRA also established the Public Works Administration (PWA), which was designed to "prime the pump" of economic recovery by stimulating the construction industry and therefore providing jobs for unemployed men. Projects were contracted out to private-sector firms, which in turn hired workers. Under the leadership of "Honest Harold" Ickes, the PWA was slow to authorize funds, and it remained a fraction of the size of the other relief programs. The Tennessee Valley Authority (TVA) set up a public corporation to construct dams for flood control and generating electricity, to manufacture fertilizer, and to build a "model city"—Norris, Tennessee. Finally, the Civilian Conservation Corps (CCC) was set up to provide work for young men in the national forests. Using camps run by the army, it paid $30 a month and enrolled between 300,000 and 500,000 men each month—a total of 2.5 million in the course of its ten-year history.

These ambitious programs were almost all designed for white men. Women were omitted entirely from the PWA, TVA, and CCC, since construction and forestry were not considered suitable activities for them. African-American men were either barred outright or marginalized through the use of quotas. For instance, in the CCC, African-American enrollment was limited

A Civilian Conservation Corps (CCC) crew planting trees in Superior National Forest, Minnesota. [National Archives]

to 10 percent of the total and the men were housed in segregated camps.[19] African-Americans were similarly restricted in the TVA and were prohibited from living in Norris. The AAA's crop reduction program took acreage out of cultivation, pushing tenant farmers and sharecroppers off their land. Government subsidy payments were usually kept by white landowners, who then used the money to purchase farm equipment, further reducing the demand for black labor. The NRA actually increased unemployment for African-Americans, who were sometimes fired when the same wages were set for blacks and whites. In addition, the codes of fair competition led to many small business failures, which disproportionately affected African-Americans, results that led some African-American leaders to call the NRA the "Negro Removal Act."[20]

The programs of the New Deal's first one-hundred days at first appeared to have stopped the economic decline. While the recovery was far from robust, the corner had been turned. In addition, these measures helped provide economic stability and the basis for the tremendous economic expansion after World War II. In fact, much of the New Deal legislation remained relatively intact until the Reagan administration's deregulation and assault on labor in the 1980s. Regulation of the banks, and of the financial sector in general, prevented a recurrence of the fiasco of the early 1930s. The AAA continues to provide subsidies to farmers. And the NIRA served as the prototype for the 1935 National Labor Relations Act, which established the National Labor Relations Board to protect the right of workers to organize unions and to have employers bargain in good faith. (We should be clear, however, that it was not the New Deal policies but the tremendous increase in government expenditures in the early 1940s that was part of the mobilization for World War II that finally ended the Depression.)

The New Deal legislation not only confirmed the government's role as a critical player in the economy, but also satisfied enough demands for reform to undermine calls for more fundamental change. For example, Bronson Cutting, Senator from New Mexico, remarked later that Roosevelt could have nationalized the banks instead of bailing them out.[21] Yet leaving the "money changers" in charge was part of the mission of rescuing capitalism.

Despite their size and number, these programs only went part of the way to solving the problem of unemployment. Approximately 12 million people were out of work when Roosevelt became president, and more and more of them were joining in protests. Furthermore, the AAA, PWA, CCC, and TVA were all aimed at white men and did not include women and African-Americans. It was clear to the Roosevelt administration that a massive relief program was needed to respond to the needs of a much larger number of people.

2

FEDERAL UNEMPLOYMENT RELIEF

The final issue addressed during of the first one-hundred days of the New Deal was relief. Although much of the business community steadfastly opposed federal unemployment relief, increasing destitution, continuing protests, the exhaustion of traditional sources of relief, and pleas from local and state governments compelled the Roosevelt administration to act. The alternative, as historian Arthur M. Schlesinger, Jr., wrote in his study of this period, might be revolution.[1]

The bill establishing the Federal Emergency Relief Administration (FERA) was signed on May 12, 1933. It was seen as a temporary measure, designed to meet an emergency need, and money was only appropriated for two years. This was clear from the introduction to the act:

The Congress hereby declares that the present economic depression has created a serious emergency, due to widespread unemployment and increasing inadequacy of State and local relief funds, resulting in the existing or threatened deprivation of a considerable number of families and individuals of the necessities of life, and making it imperative that the Federal Government cooperate more effectively with the several States and Territories and the District of Columbia in furnishing relief to the needy and distressed people.[2]

The programs established under the FERA had two goals that were considered critical if the program was to work. The first was to counteract the "ideology of the dole"—the belief that receiving relief was in some way shameful—so that large numbers of people would apply. The second was to restore the "work ethic," which the government believed had been weakened after so many years of unemployment. Therefore the focus was on *work relief,* although it was to be voluntary work—to distinguish it from the forced character of the old "work-tests." The work itself was to be as much like "real work" as possible: payments were to be based on the type of work performed, people were to be paid in cash rather than in kind, and the work was to be useful—unlike the stigmatizing make-work of previous programs.

In terms of structure, the FERA was to provide grants to State Emergency Relief Administrations (SERAs), which would in turn distribute them to local agencies. The local agencies were actually to give out the money, either as work relief or direct relief (with no additional work required). Most of the work projects were therefore developed by local agencies. Initially, the FERA was given $250 million to allocate directly and another $250 million to allocate as "one-to-three" matching grants—the FERA would provide $1 for every $3 provided by the states. In order to receive federal monies, the SERAs were required to follow rules and regulations developed by FERA administrators. If they failed to do so, funds could be temporarily held up, and in cases considered sufficiently serious the state relief administration could be taken over, or federalized, by the FERA.

A FERA construction project to build the Maine State Pier. [National Archives]

Eligibility was based on need. Each family or individual that applied had to pass a "means-test," which involved an investigation by a social worker from the local relief department. The first detailed list of regulations issued by the FERA stated that the investigation was to include at least the following:

A prompt visit to the home; inquiry as to the real property, bank accounts, and other financial resources of the family; an interview with at least one recent employer; and a determination of the ability and agreement of family, relatives, friends, and churches and other organizations to assist.[3]

It also called for visits to the recipient's home at least once a month "in order to established the continued need of those who are receiving relief."[4] A family's income (from all sources) was subtracted from the amount the local relief agency determined it needed, and the resulting "budgetary deficiency" was provided as relief.

Not surprisingly, such stringent procedures were difficult to follow and left a great deal of room for local variation. Josephine C. Brown, who was a program administrator at the time, wrote that the most important factors were the availability of funds, the size of the rolls, the local attitude toward relief, and the local standard of living.[5] In general, the means-test was applied most leniently in the large northern cities, where protest was more widespread, as the high levels of unemployment led people to understand that joblessness was not caused by personal failure but by factors beyond the control of individuals. It was applied most stringently in the rural areas of the south, where the white elite continued to fight attempts to provide relief, especially to African-Americans, because it also provided an alternative to low-wage labor.

Federal funds were supposed to be directed to people who were considered "employable"—those the government would otherwise expect to have jobs. Those considered "unemployable" were supposed to be cared for with local funds. But the continuing shortfall in tax revenues, along with the sustained clamor for aid among the unemployed, forced federal officials to provide some direct relief. "Unemployables" therefore made up approximately 20 percent of the FERA's relief rolls.[6]

WOMEN AND AFRICAN-AMERICANS AS SECOND-CLASS CITIZENS

Women and people of color, particularly African-Americans, had difficulty receiving relief under the FERA. Women had trouble because eligibility was limited to one member of a family—the one designated head of household—and this was inevitably the man (if one was present). The only exception to the "one member per family" rule was for young people, who could participate in the CCC and the College Student Aid Program even if an adult family member was working on a FERA program.[7] Women also had a hard time finding work placements since they were excluded from construction projects, which provided most of the work. They were thus confined to white-collar projects, such as teaching and secretarial work, if they had professional or clerical skills, or production-for-use projects in which consumer goods were made for distribution to others on relief.

African-Americans had an even harder time. Although FERA regulations forbade racial discrimination, African-Americans experienced difficulties establishing eligibility, were paid lower rates, and were usually assigned to unskilled, manual labor. Proving eligibility was the first hurdle. First, since African-Americans generally earned less than whites, relief workers assumed they needed less income. They therefore had to be poorer than whites to qualify. And second, it was difficult for African-Americans to stay on the rolls because they were required to accept low-wage private sector jobs that were considered unsuitable for whites. This disparity was seen in direct relief payments as well. A study of several counties in the south found that while white families were allocated an average of $12.65 a month, black families only received $8.31.[8]

Even when African-Americans established eligibility, they had difficulty finding work placements, especially ones that matched their skills, since stereotypes of what constituted "appropriate" work for different groups were built into the programs. Skilled black workers were often classified as unskilled, regardless of their occupation, and paid the lowest rates. Throughout the 1930s, African-Americans complained that men who were skilled masons and carpenters and women who were clerical workers were given work digging ditches and doing other manual labor. Sometimes they would be sent to a project, only to have the sponsoring agency turn them away, or insist they only do unskilled work. In addition, whites were often assigned to supervise black projects. Finally, almost all of the projects were racially segregated, and

**Women at work on a FERA garden project near Savannah, Georgia.
[National Archives]**

relief administrators had difficulty finding sponsors for projects involving black workers. African-American men worked in segregated construction gangs, while African-American women made clothes in segregated sewing rooms; even the transient camps were segregated. Conditions for African-Americans were almost always worse than those for whites. African-American women continued to face both color and gender discrimination and few received help under FERA.[9]

WHITE-COLLAR WORKERS
RECEIVE PREFERENTIAL TREATMENT

"White-collar workers" were given preferential treatment on

the FERA projects. Relief officials, concerned about high unemployment among formerly middle-class professional and other nonmanual workers, as well as about their reluctance to ask for "relief," developed policies designed to entice them onto the rolls. They made the relief investigation relatively simple and directed that "in determining budgetary needs, the previous standard of living may be taken into account," which effectively raised their wage rates, and sometimes hours worked, and therefore the total amount they could earn.[10] Relief officials also designed special types of work, in what were called white-collar projects, or professional and nonmanual projects. White women were included in this category, and made up one-third of all those on the professional and nonmanual projects. African-Americans were almost entirely excluded, comprising only 5 percent of the white-collar rolls throughout the FERA.[11]

WAGE-RATE POLICIES

The FERA policy on wage rates and hours was first set forth in July 1933, part of a long and detailed list of regulations. It specified that people on work relief should receive a "fair rate of pay for work performed," generally the prevailing market wage for similar work. Skilled workers were to receive "skilled wages."[12] Once a family's "budgetary deficiency" was determined, this amount was divided by the appropriate wage rate to determine the number of hours of work a family member would be given. (For example, if a family's budgetary deficiency was determined to be $10.00 per week and the person on relief was classified as earning a wage of $.50 cents per hour, she or he could work 20 hours a week.)

This fair-wage policy was announced on July 11. Ten days later it was altered. In what was to become one of the most contentious of all FERA decisions, relief administrators set a minimum relief rate of $.30 per hour.[13] In other words, no one on work relief could be paid less than this, no matter what the prevailing rate was in the area. Relief administrators wanted to boost both relief payments and extremely low wages, primarily in southern and rural areas. They feared that wage rates in the private sector were often so low—in rural areas of the south they averaged between $.10 and $.125 per hour—that relief rates would be equally low. (In addition, maximum hours of work were set: no one could work more than 35 hours a week if they were manual laborers, or 40 hours a week if they were office workers.)

Average work relief payments increased slowly in the wake of this policy, rising by one-third over the next three months. Yet payments still remained low, about $17 a month in October, the month before the FERA was interrupted by the CWA.[14] As we will see, average payments received a great boost from the CWA, and after the FERA was resumed the following April payments remained 50 to 80 percent higher than they had been in October 1933.

While FERA administrators wanted to raise wage rates in general, they made no attempt to reduce the differentials in wages between women and men or between blacks and whites. On the contrary, dual wage scales based on both gender and race were often adopted formally by relief agencies. This practice was not uncommon at the time: for instance, many local governments paid different wages to black and white teachers and nurses.[15] In addition, the NRA's own code of fair competition allowed lower wages for women. An NRA official justified this policy, explaining that "Numerous differentials of various kinds can be found in the codes which it may be difficult to defend on purely logical grounds, but they represent long established customs."[16]

The minimum work relief wage-rate policy provoked vehement protests from business, so intense that the rate was terminated in November 1934. Those in the south argued that African-Americans were leaving their jobs to work on government programs—even though blacks faced such serious obstacles finding FERA work that the prospect of a labor shortage was more a fear than a reality. Yet for many southern whites *any* relief for

Men at work in a FERA typesetting and printing project. [National Archives]

African-Americans was too much relief. Some states went so far as to close their programs rather than pay the $.30 per hour minimum. The North Carolina Emergency Relief Commission, for example, ended its work program in all but a few cities because "this [minimum] wage was much above the level of wages in practically all sections of the state."[17]

Despite the minimum, the wages earned by workers both on the FERA and in the private sector were sometimes so low that they had to be supplemented with direct relief. This was particularly true for large families whose budgetary deficiency was often greater than the amount they earned on work relief. Yet relief administrators were reluctant to supplement work relief payments, believing that if payments were based on need rather than work performed, the sense that work relief was a "real job" would be undermined. They also opposed supplementing private sector wages because this would encourage employers to pay lower wages—knowing that relief would fill the gap. Despite their protests, however, necessity prevailed and supplementation continued. A May 1934 survey found that at least one-fourth of all those on FERA work relief were paid such low wages that they received direct relief as well.[18]

DIVERSIFYING FERA PROJECTS

During the early FERA most of the projects were continuations of existing local work relief. They were therefore primarily in construction: repairing roads, public buildings, and other facilities; new construction of small facilities; and maintenance, e.g., cleaning streets and raking leaves in parks. The FERA also continued production-for-use projects, in which people on relief made consumer goods that were distributed to others on relief or used in other work projects or in public institutions. These included subsistence gardens, projects to can and preserve produce, and fuel procurement, primarily chopping wood in woodyards. The major type of production-for-use, however, was workrooms in which women sewed and mended garments and made bedding and other articles. Such "labor-intensive workrooms," where the women either sewed by hand or used old-fashioned treadle machines, had been introduced during the depressions of the late 1800s and were an accepted form of relief for women. Although some people criticized the workrooms as little more than sweatshops, they provided the main type of work relief for blue-collar women. Furthermore, although they were segregated, the sewing rooms furnished most of the work relief for African-American women. The women produced a wide range of goods: they made dresses, hospital supplies, rag rugs, pillow cases, sheets, towels, and mattresses; they renovated clothing and hats; they spun wool into yarn and then made socks and blankets; and they quilted.[19]

As the FERA got underway, additional projects were developed to meet the needs of specific segments of the population and to address situations that warranted special attention. In the first few months, divisions were set up to deal with transients, the self-help cooperatives that had been established during the early years of the Depression, teachers, women, and drought relief. In addition, the Federal Surplus Relief Corporation (FSRC) was established to procure surplus commodities for families on relief.

Transients received immediate attention because of the visibility of their distress. The proliferation of Hoovervilles and the attack on the Bonus Army the previous summer had made the entire country aware of their plight. Since residence requirements prevented transients from receiving relief if they left their home states, few were getting aid when the FERA began. Thus the Transient Program quickly set up shelters in the cities (usually in renovated factories or warehouses) and camps in the countryside where people received food, clothing, and a place to sleep. The camps required work in exchange for relief—the closest the FERA came to a work-test. Beginning with the 67,000 individuals and families who were already receiving some state or local aid, the Transient Program slowly expanded so that by February 1935 approximately 300,000 cases were receiving relief. But the conditions in the shelters and camps were often depressing, food was insufficient, and people's movement and activities were restricted. Single women and families, the subject of greater national concern, tended to receive better treatment than single men.[20]

In addition, some transients were excluded. Wary of creating more problems by competing with the low-wage sectors of the economy than was already the case, federal relief officials specified that although seamen could be classified as transients, seasonal migrant workers could not.[21] Instead, the states and the workers' employers were expected to care for them. What this

Women using treadle sewing machines to make clothing for families on relief. [National Archives]

meant was that migrant workers remained available for work in agriculture at very low rates.

A special division was also established to provide aid to the self-help cooperatives. While these worked well when prices for agricultural goods had been so depressed that farmers were willing to trade their crops for labor services, the success of the AAA's program to increase the price of agricultural commodities meant that the farmers were no longer willing to continue these barter arrangements. Thus the FERA provided relief funds to help the cooperatives turn to the production of other goods and services, with the clear requirement that nothing they produced could be sold through normal market channels. By 1934 cooperatives throughout the country were engaged in a wide variety of activities.

SELF-HELP COOPERATIVE ACITIVITIES

- **LANDSCAPE GARDENING**
- **FARM LABOR**
- **BUTCHERING**
- **RAISING POULTRY AND RABBITS**
- **CANNING FRUITS AND VEGETABLES**
- **PLUMBING**
- **FISHING**
- **GRINDING GRAIN**
- **LOGGING**
- **CARPENTRY**
- **HOUSE REPAIR**
- **HOUSE WRECKING**
- **DENTISTRY**
- **PRINTING**
- **BAKING**
- **BROOM MAKING**
- **MAKING BEDDING**
- **MAKING CRATES**
- **CIDER MAKING**
- **SEWING**
- **TAILORING**
- **UPHOLSTERING AND FURNITURE REPAIR**
- **MAKING MAPLE SYRUP**
- **PICKLING**
- **RUG MAKING**
- **REPAIRING SHOES**
- **REPAIRING RADIOS**
- **REPAIRING APPLIANCES**
- **RUNNING COMMISSARIES, CAFETERIAS, BEAUTY SHOPS, BARBER SHOPS, COAL**

Federal aid was given to the cooperatives through the fall of 1935, with approximately 30,000 people participating in them during this two-year period.[22] But as we will see in Chapter 5, aid to the cooperatives was gradually restricted in response to business complaints that the federal government was funding projects in competition with the private sector. This also held true for other innovative production-for-use projects.

Another group in need of aid was teachers. The decline in tax revenues during the early years of the Depression had led to a shorter school year for many schools, while others had closed entirely, especially in rural communities. Tens of thousands of teachers had lost their jobs. The Emergency Education Program, which was started in October, was designed to provide work for some of these unemployed teachers. But FERA administrators were determined that work relief should not replace normal government operations—they were fearful that local governments would abrogate their responsibility for education, increasing the relief rolls by replacing employed teachers with those on relief. Relief funds were therefore used to operate elementary and secondary schools only in rural areas (those with populations under 5,000) through the Rural School Continuation Program, but not in large communities. Thus although at its height in March 1935 the Emergency Education Program provided work for more than 44,000 teachers, most were teaching adults. There were classes in general adult education (the largest component), literacy, vocational education, vocational rehabilitation, parent education (homemaking, child guidance, etc.). There was also a small program in worker education, which provided jobs for almost 600 teachers and enrolled more than 255,000 people, focussing on adults who had received little prior schooling and stressing workplace and social problems and their relation to workers' lives. In addition, nursery schools were opened for children from relief families.[23]

Other projects were developed for professional and non-manual workers. Beginning on a small scale, they were expanded throughout the 1930s and have become some of the best-known projects. In the early FERA these white-collar projects included: doing clerical work for government agencies and institutions; working in libraries, museums, and art galleries; operating recreation programs; nursing and other health care; conducting a

Members of the Washington, D.C., Self-Help Cooperative unloading donated firewood for distribution. [National Archives]

variety of surveys and research for FERA; and arts projects for musicians and muralists.[24]

Many women received work through the Emergency Education Program. However, since they were excluded from manual labor on construction projects, this did not go very far in meeting their needs. Recognizing this, in September FERA administrators set up a Women's Work division to develop projects considered particularly appropriate for women. It also established a Drought Relief Program to help people affected by the drought that was turning much of the Midwest into a dustbowl. The program provided funds to construct "feeder" roads, as well as to provide food and clothing for poor families and feed for their livestock, and was expanded in the spring of 1934 when production-for-use projects were set up to process cattle dying from the drought.[26] Finally, the Federal Surplus Relief Corporation (FRSC) was established to deal with the enormous agricultural surpluses that were being produced at the same time that people were starving. In the summer of 1933 the public had been outraged when the AAA instructed farmers to plow under 25 percent of the cotton crop and to kill over 6 million piglets and sows in order to increase the prices of cotton and pork products. Thus the FSRC used some of the agricultural surpluses collected by the AAA more productively—to feed people—while still boosting prices. Taking these surplus goods off the market, they were distributed as in-kind relief or processed in work-relief projects (primarily production-for-use) and then distributed to relief recipients. In addition, the FSRC authorized the use of surplus commodities to feed needy children in schools, an initiative that later became the school lunch program.[27]

As we will see in Chapter 5, many of these projects incurred the wrath of the business sector, which saw them as encroachments on their terrain.

3

THE CIVIL WORKS ADMINISTRATION: ANTIDOTE TO A DEPRESSION WINTER

As the first winter of the New Deal approached, Roosevelt and his advisors worried that the FERA would not be able to meet the demand for relief. Cold weather had led to an upsurge of protest in previous winters, and there was no reason to assume that this one would be different. Despite the NRA and PWA, which had led to a spurt in economic activity between March and June, the economy had resumed its downward slide.[1] Almost one-fourth of the labor force was still unemployed. State and local government revenues remained low, and many counties, cities, and towns had declared bankruptcy.[2]

Needing something grand to meet this crisis, the Civil Works

A 1933 march of the unemployed in Los Angeles demanding milk for children and an end to evictions. [AP/Wide World Photos]

Administration (CWA) was developed. Established on November 9, 1933, by executive order under the authority of the NIRA, it was supposed to provide work quickly for 4 million unemployed people. In order to gear the program up, projects and personnel were transferred from the FERA and the states were encouraged to develop projects with the threat that they would lose any funds not put to use by December 15.[3]

Since the CWA's enabling legislation was under the NIRA, as was the PWA, its regulations superseded those of the FERA. This led to two critical differences that made the CWA seem much more like "real jobs" rather than work relief. First, the 2 million new additions to the work program were exempted from a means-test. In effect, their status as unemployed served as a sufficient test of their neediness. As relief chief Harry Hopkins explained, "We are licked before we start if this is confined entirely to the relief rolls. It is telling every man [sic] unemployed ... who fought this battle through from the beginning on his own, that he has to get on the relief rolls before he can get a job."[4] Second, since a means-test was not used to determine eligibility, payments could not be based on budgetary deficiency. Instead, all CWA participants were paid according to the higher PWA wage-rate scales, including a $.40 per hour minimum.

The CWA retains the distinction of providing work for more people at any one time than any other voluntary program in U.S. history—more than 4.3 million at its height in January 1934, with another 100,000 on FERA work relief. Yet the demand for jobs was so great that another 7 million applied but were not accepted. City halls in New England were mobbed by CWA applicants. In New York City, thousands of people lined up outside employment offices shortly after midnight the day before applications were accepted, and the city was forced to set up branch offices in settlement houses and welfare organizations to handle the crowds. In some cities, lotteries were used to determine who would get the CWA jobs. In Chicago, for instance, 300,000 men drew lots for 49,000 positions. Preference was given to World War I veterans with dependents.[5] The mayor of Chelsea, Massachusetts, told Hopkins that the 2,000 applicants for 155 positions had "congregated sullenly" and might well turn into a mob. And a riot ensued in Dayton, Tennessee, when 2,000 people applied for 299 positions. In a panic, the government temporarily withdrew all CWA work.[6]

WOMEN AND THE CIVIL WORKS SERVICE

Hopkins' statement that *men* should be exempted from the means-test was not an error of language: the CWA was designed primarily for male heads of household and most women were excluded. Since CWA money came from the same source as PWA funds, it could only be used for construction projects, which were not considered suitable for women. However, women's need for relief had become the subject of increasing attention. At a Conference on the Emergency Needs of Women, held at the White House in November—with Eleanor Roosevelt presiding—Harry Hopkins set a target of bringing between 300,000 and 400,000 women into either CWA or FERA programs, and participants discussed the types of projects that could be developed.[7]

Three days later, the Civil Works Service (CWS) was established to provide work relief through white-collar and production-for-use projects. It remained under the FERA, rather than the CWA, which meant that a means-test was still used to determine eligibility and that payments were based on the prevailing wage rate with only a $.30 an hour minimum (i.e., the FERA wage scale).[8]

While the treatment of blue-collar women under the CWS continued as it had in the FERA, an important advance was made for professional and nonmanual workers. Rather than undergoing the rigorous investigation prescribed by FERA, they could be certified as eligible by committees from professional organizations. Although this policy was justified by federal relief officials as a way to "reduce case investigations," it was also intended to reduce the stigma of relief for white-collar workers. Yet projects were not set up quickly enough, and Hopkins' target was never met. Although almost 1 million women applied, only 217,000 were accepted—a mere 5 percent of the total CWA and CWS rolls.[9]

THE CWA BEGINS QUICKLY

Once the CWA was announced, relief administrators faced the daunting task of beginning projects that would provide work for more than 2 million additional people before winter set in. Projects not only had to be developed quickly, but they were mandated to be "economically and socially desirable." At the

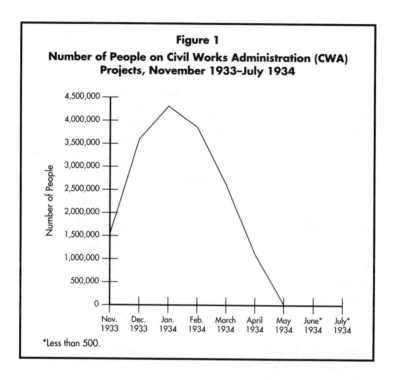

Figure 1

Number of People on Civil Works Administration (CWA) Projects, November 1933–July 1934

*Less than 500.

same time, a "maximum of human labor" had to be used in lieu of machinery "wherever practicable."[10] This last requirement inevitably led some of the projects to look like make-work. In addition, there were problems securing enough tools for such a huge number of people—yet without tools, little work could be done.[11]

These problems, and the program's own mandates, were met most easily in projects that involved repairing public property, although there was also some new construction, primarily roads and small public facilities. Thus construction projects consumed almost 90 percent of CWA funds and included repairing almost 242,000 miles of roads (and building another 13,000 miles); improving hundreds of schools and other public buildings, sewers and water works; and constructing recreational facilities (e.g., swimming pools, athletic stadiums, and community centers) and more than 450 landing fields at municipal airports.[12]

Professional and nonmanual projects in the arts, education, and research expanded from their small base in the early FERA and received almost 6 percent of CWA funds. The education programs were essentially a continuation of the FERA Emergency Education Program to employ teachers in relief nursery schools and in a variety of adult education classes. There were archaeological excavations of Native American sites and surveys of historical buildings. And a Public Works of Art Project was started, providing work for about 3,000 artists, painters, sculptors, etchers, and muralists. These were the projects that were most often attacked as unnecessary boondoggles, a reaction that reflected a very narrow view of the proper role of government. But relief officials refused to cave in to such criticisms, and, as we shall see in the Chapter 6, art projects were expanded under the WPA, providing work for professionals and entertainment for the public.[13]

Another 3 percent of the funds were used for public welfare and health activities, which ranged from white-collar projects for health care workers to serving lunches to children in relief-sponsored nursery schools. Finally, a scant 1 percent of the funds went to production-for-use projects that were continued from the early FERA, including the sewing rooms, fuel procurement, and the gardening and canning projects. In addition, projects to process (slaughter and preserve) animals dying from the drought were established when the CWA began.[14]

Finally, the College Student Aid (CSA) program was established in February 1934 to provide part-time work relief for needy college students at rates "commonly paid by the college or university," again with a $.30 per hour minimum. Apparently, it was considered important to keep these aspiring middle-class students in school and out of the wider labor force.[15]

Civil Works Administration (CWA) workers laying sewer pipes in Wisconsin. [National Archives]

PAYMENTS UNDER THE CWA

Adoption of the PWA wage-rate scale under the CWA was a boon to workers. Using the PWA system, states were classified into three zones, each of which had a different minimum hourly rate, as follows: in the Southern zone, $1.00 for skilled workers and $.40 for unskilled workers; in the Central zone, $1.10 for skilled workers and $.45 for unskilled workers; and in the Northern zone, $1.20 for skilled workers and $.50 for unskilled workers. If wage rates under collective bargaining agreements or understandings between workers and employers were higher than the minimums in a particular community, the higher rates were to be used. And no one could work more than thirty hours a week, as was also the case under the PWA. As a result, average payments nationally to people on the work programs more than tripled, increasing from $17 per month in October 1933—before the CWA began—to $60 per month at its height in January 1934.[16]

But the business community complained. In response to their criticisms, the relatively high CWA rates were defended by Harry Hopkins in Congressional hearings:

> I have a feeling that the wage scale is not too high; that the people who want to lower the scale and bring it down are people who have maintained their existence through the payment of low wages; that if the new conditions mean anything it means a larger distribution of this world's goods in the hands of the workers, and an adequate or sufficient wage scale.[17]

Perhaps anticipating these complaints, not all CWA workers were paid according to the higher rates. The $.40 an hour minimum did not extend to road projects, which retained the $.30 minimum, apparently because of the strong opposition to paying the higher minimum rate to unskilled workers, many of whom were African-American. The lower rate was also retained in the CWS, and although federal relief officials argued that this was necessary because the CWS was part of the FERA, not the CWA, it had the effect of helping preserve the wage differential between women and men.[18]

In general, treatment of African-Americans on the CWA was as discriminatory as it had been in the FERA. Blacks, including those who were skilled laborers or white-collar workers, were invariably classified as unskilled. Pay differentials were continued, sometimes overtly. In Houston, Texas, for instance, white teachers earned $1.00 per hour, while African-American teachers earned only $.60 per hour. In Jackson, Mississippi, black men who were supposed to receive $.40 cents per hour were paid only $.30.[19] Evangelist John R. Perkins expressed their ire in a poem:

> We received our work cards marked 40 cents per hour
> And went to work without any regret
> On Saturday two hundred colored men was deceived
> And 30 cents was all we could get...

We only want Uncle Sam to know
They did not treat us right
They cut our wages to 30 cents per hour
Yet 40 cents was paid to the white.[20]

REACTIONS TO THE CWA

The CWA was created to develop jobs quickly, and by December there were 180,000 CWA projects across the nation. The program was greeted with great enthusiasm by workers, New Deal and local government officials, liberals and progressives, all of whom who praised it for creating jobs and putting money in people's pockets. And retail merchants were pleased because CWA workers spent their earnings on low-priced consumer goods.[21]

CWA administrators were flooded with letters and telegrams commending them for paying "wages" instead of a "dole," for their "untiring efforts in creating worthwhile projects," and for their speed in putting so many people to work in time for the holidays. A typical letter came from George P. Griffith, president of the Bricklayers' International Union of Alabama, who wrote to Harry Hopkins from Birmingham:

> Our sincere thanks for your splendid organization and speed of the CWA, making it possible for our members to have employment in time to earn some Christmas money and provide some pleasure for our loved ones. In this City, the spirit seemed to equal the spirit shown in 1929; streets and stores full of shoppers.[22]

And Arthur "Tex" Goldschmidt, CWA assistant administrator, spoke for many when he said the CWA "just started everything."[23]

But support was far from unanimous. Most businesspeople were vehemently critical. They felt that the CWA wages were often higher than those in the private sector, drawing workers away and putting pressure on them to raise their own rates—and in fact this was probably the case.[24] They also complained that the entire program was so expensive that it would lead to huge budget deficits, which would be a serious block to economic recovery; that the projects were only make-work and were riddled with graft and corruption; that the projects were inefficient and the work could be done better by private enterprise; and that the entire relief system was undermining the confidence of the business sector and discouraging private initiative. In other words, they threatened that production and employment would stagnate if the CWA continued.[25]

Many progressives and rank-and-file workers also criticized the CWA—for not doing enough. Editorials in the *Nation* proclaimed that CWA wages were too low and that the work was "farcical," at best only "a civilized form of unemployment relief."[26] A coalition of labor groups in Pennsylvania complained about the types of work given to CWA workers:

> The present Civil Works Program is using considerable money for luxuries such as bridle paths, and airports. This is not the time for luxuries. The unemployed have real needs. They should be met first.[27]

Federal relief officials quickly capitulated to this barrage of criticism. Plans to make the CWA permanent were scuttled and the existing program was cut back. A January 18 directive—to take effect the next day—cut the maximum number of hours most people could work to 24 per week in cities with populations over 2,500 and 15 per week elsewhere, and it was announced that the entire program would soon be ended.[28] The cuts in hours were, in effect, a way to reduce total wages, and people's paychecks fell an average of 25 percent in the following week.[29] Only white-collar supervisory, clerical, and professional workers were exempted, although the greater militancy among the unemployed in the northern cities resulted in a smaller decline in hours in these areas.

The announcement that CWA projects would be closed down elicited a torrent of protest. Elected officials, from members of

Men in a worker education project studying algebra. [National Archives]

Congress to mayors, urged that it be continued. There were protest demonstrations in many cities, including Washington, D.C., Minneapolis, and New York. And Congress received 37,000 letters in just one week in late January supporting the CWA. Many of those who had criticized the program for doing too little nevertheless wanted it to continue, fearing a return to the relief programs of the early FERA, with the means-test, lower payments, and fewer jobs. As *Time* magazine reported in February, "The wave of complaints against the way the CWA was run was only a mild ripple compared to the comber [sic] of complaints against the plan to stop running the CWA altogether." Some people thought that the announcement was just a government maneuver, "a political statement, intended to curb excesses."[30]

Despite the protests, the government proceeded to dissolve the program. Dismantling began in the South, where less organizing among the unemployed made this process easier. Wage cuts were mandated in early March, when PWA wage rates were dropped and the old FERA scales were reinstituted. Personnel and most of the projects were transferred from the CWA to FERA work programs. The CWA, a compromise between a relief and an employment program, was replaced by a program that was, once again, purely relief.

4

THE NEW FERA: THE EMERGENCY WORK RELIEF PROGRAM OF 1934-1935

As the CWA was dismantled, work programs again became the responsibility of the FERA, which now incorporated many of the lessons learned during the previous year. All participants had to meet a means-test. Budgetary deficiency was reintroduced and the $.30 per hour minimum wage rate was reinstated. Charges of inefficiency and make-work led to the expansion of production-for-use projects, while an effort was made to entice more professional and nonmanual workers into the programs, and new projects were set up to make use of their skills. This helped women, but virtually nothing was done to deal with the blatant discrimination against African-Americans.

In order to deal more effectively with the different problems of the urban and rural poor, the FERA was now divided into two programs—the Rural Rehabilitation Program (RRP) for rural areas and small towns, and the Emergency Work Relief Program (EWRP) for the unemployed in the cities and predominantly urban areas. The RRP was the smaller of the two, with only 200,000 families enrolled by April 1935. It was designed to put "the individual family in a position to become self-supporting," and developed work projects as well as distributing direct relief. The plan was to let people who lived on good or fair land be "rehabilitated in place," while those on submarginal land or in "stranded communities"—small towns that were dependent on a single industry that had closed—were to be moved to new communities.[1]

DISCRIMINATION AND SPECIAL PROGRAMS

The main component of the new FERA was the EWRP. In setting up this program, relief officials tried to meet some of the criticisms of the CWA and the early FERA, as well as to develop policies and projects that would draw in people who had previously been reluctant participants, primarily white-collar workers. Thus while a rigorous investigation by a social worker was the norm for manual laborers, this was not the case for white-collar workers, who went to special relief offices set up just for them. FERA administrator Josephine C. Brown explained that this allowed white-collar workers to "avoid incurring the stigma of mingling with 'ordinary' relief applicants."[2] The less intrusive relief investigation used during the CWA was continued, as spelled out in a July 1934 regulation: "Eligibility for employment [of white-collar workers in work-relief programs] will be established by means of a questionnaire filled by the applicant and verified by a professional or technical organization or by a case worker."[3] A month later, the onus was further eased: professional and manual workers had to be eligible for relief, but they did not have to actually be on the rolls in order to participate.

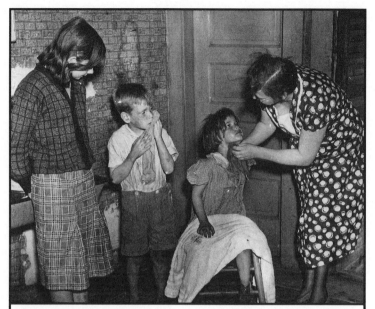

A woman in a FERA program cares for orphaned children in their home. [National Archives]

They were to be given continuous work, without having to take time off the program if their project ended, and there was to be only a minimum of follow-up. In addition, their budgets were to be high enough not only to provide for "health, decency, and comfort," but also to be "commensurate with the previous standard of living."[4]

While women's needs for relief were given special attention through the Women's Division that had been set up in October 1933, policies developed slowly and only one-fifth of the more than 1 million women who applied for the CWA and CWS had been given work. The most important obstacles were the reluctance of local relief workers to certify women as eligible for relief if a man still lived in the home and the lack of suitable projects for women. Therefore, federal relief administrators tried to develop work relief projects designed specifically for women. This included the projects for white-collar workers, which provided work for almost one-third of all women on the FERA.[5] In addition, FERA officials periodically encouraged state and local relief administrations to provide more work for women in white-collar as well as other projects. Yet no sanctions were imposed if women were not given work, and the number of women in the program still grew slowly compared to the number of men—from 109,000, or 8 percent of the rolls, in May 1934, to a high of 298,000, or 12 percent of the rolls, the following March.[6]

There was no similar effort to reverse the racial discrimination of the early FERA and the CWA. African-Americans were still assumed to need less income than whites, still classified as unskilled no matter what their real skill levels, and still had a more difficult time establishing eligibility. While FERA officials believed that promoting work for women was important enough to warrant a Women's Division, there was no analogous program for blacks, a clear signal of federal tolerance of racial discrimination. Furthermore, although federal relief administrators sometimes called upon the SERAs to provide more work for African-Americans, especially professionals, their own racist attitudes were often apparent in the wording of the directives. For example, in the fall of 1934 FERA officials responded to complaints of racial discrimination by reminding the SERAs to use black physicians, dentists, and pharmacists to provide medical relief for other African-Americans, but to do this only "so far as economic limitations and the maintenance of efficient service will allow."[7]

The fact that African-Americans were overrepresented on the relief rolls compared to their total numbers in the population reflected their dire straits in the 1930s—particularly given the fact that they had so much trouble getting on the rolls in the first place (especially in rural areas). While blacks comprised 9.7 percent of the total population, a May 1934 survey of urban workers on relief (in 79 cities) found that they comprised 18.9 percent of the urban relief rolls, while whites made up 78.6 percent and people of other races filled the remaining 2.5 percent.[8]

Another program that grew under the EWRP was the Transient Program, which almost doubled, from 105,000 cases in March 1934 to a high of almost 200,000 the following winter. Although this meant that a large proportion of transient families received relief, their situation was still far from secure.[9]

WAGE AND HOUR POLICIES

As we saw in the last chapter, by the end of the CWA work-relief wage rates had been reduced back to the original FERA levels. These rates were maintained in the EWRP: payments were based on a family's budgetary deficiency, which was divided by the prevailing wage rate for the type of work performed to determine the hours a person could work. The minimum wage returned to $.30 per hour, and the maximum number of hours a person could work in any week was twenty-four. In order to avoid some of the inefficiency caused by the continual rotation of workers created by this limitation in hours, federal relief officials set a minimum of fifty-four hours per month for unskilled workers and thirty hours per month for all others. However, as a result, the hours allowed for many skilled workers in low-budget states were below this amount—i.e., their monthly budgetary deficiency divided by their wage rate was less than the thirty-hour minimum. Therefore, they were eliminated from the work program altogether and received direct relief instead.[10]

Determining the prevailing wage rates was sometimes controversial, and the FERA's solution reflected the interests of the groups that developed the NRA's codes of fair competition. It was also testimony to the struggles over the level of work-relief wage rates, as the business sector argued for lower rates while organized labor fought for higher rates. Thus prevailing rates were to be determined by local committees that had one representative from labor, one from business, and one from the relief administration. If there were already "wage agreements or understandings between local labor organizations and employers in the locality," these were to become the prevailing rates. However, since the committees had no power to enforce their decisions, they became little more than fact-finding bodies. If a committee's decisions were not unanimous, the rates would be determined by a grievance committee, also made up of representatives from business, labor, and government. And in some areas, there were no committees at all.[11]

As in the early FERA and the CWA, EWRP wage differentials reflected those in the broader society, and were based on gender, race, and class. Yet on the whole workers fared better in this phase of the FERA than they had earlier. Most importantly, although on average workers only earned half what they had on the CWA, this was still more than twice what they had earned under the early FERA.[12]

DEVELOPING NEW PROJECTS

Innovative new projects were developed in the EWRP in response to criticisms of the earlier work programs and in order to meet the needs of different populations of unemployed. The complaint that the programs provided merely inefficient and unnecessary make-work led to mandates to develop projects that would be of "economic and social benefit to the general public" and "carefully planned to be of the greatest efficiency." In order to avoid replacing workers who would normally be employed, projects were also supposed to be "apart from normal government enterprises." Thus maintenance projects were prohibited—specifically garbage collection, snow removal, street cleaning, and lawn maintenance in parks. (It is noteworthy that although maintenance work was often denounced as a boondoggle, in fact it was necessary work that would otherwise have been done by regularly employed government workers. It is analogous

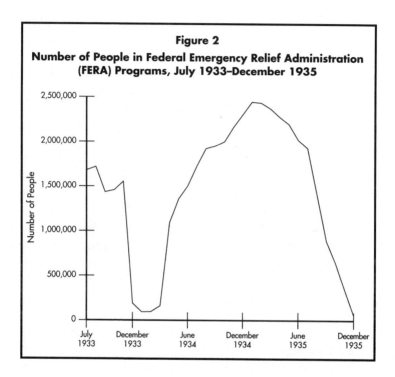

Figure 2
Number of People in Federal Emergency Relief Administration (FERA) Programs, July 1933–December 1935

to housework—usually noticed only when it is not done.) To make the programs more efficient, it was decided to allow up to 10 percent of project workers to be hired directly instead of taking them from the relief rolls: it was hoped that this would make it possible to hire more skilled and supervisory labor.[13]

But inefficiency was built into the programs. In order to create as much work as possible with the allocated funds, projects were mandated to use a maximum of labor and a minimum of machinery. For example, in most of the road projects this meant that instead of using grading and paving machines and only a few workers, there were many workers using simple tools, often picks and shovels. In fact, the CWA had been able to quickly provide work for an additional 2 million men since most of them worked on these labor-intensive construction projects. Clearly these projects were inefficient compared to private industry. But they followed a different logic—a "work program efficiency"—based on meeting people's need for work.[14]

Projects involving construction and repair of public property conformed to this logic. Not only were they relatively easy to develop, but they also had tangible results and provided work for millions of men. Thus they absorbed approximately 70 percent of all EWRP funds, 40 percent of which went to the construction and repair of more than 274,000 miles of road, primarily unpaved farm-to-market and other secondary roads, as well as primary roads, sidewalks, curbs, paths, and culverts. Other projects included construction of 4,700 parks, 10,900 playgrounds and athletic fields, and more than 62,000 public buildings, including schools, courthouses, firehouses, aircraft hangars, armories, sewer systems, water purification and supply systems, and airports and other transportation facilities.[15]

Although projects for professional and nonmanual workers were routinely criticized as make-work, federal relief administrators considered bringing more white-collar workers into the work program so important that these projects were significantly expanded under the EWRP, and took about 11 percent of the funds. Projects were established in public health, recreation, libraries, museums, and the arts, and provided work for nurses, doctors, dietitians, artists, writers, musicians, actors, librarians, and general clerical workers. Some white-collar workers were given the task of conducting surveys: they studied the need for relief among various groups in the population (e.g., transients, rural families, youths) and the effects of EWRP programs, made surveys of historical buildings, and developed the oral histories of former slaves that became an invaluable resource for historians.[16]

Public welfare projects were also expanded in the EWRP. Some of these projects, such as operating community centers and park recreation programs, were carried out by white-collar workers. Others were intended for blue-collar women, including the school lunch program and the housekeeping aide project, in which women were sent to help needy families in their homes.[17]

THE EXPANSION OF PRODUCTION-FOR-USE

It was difficult to respond to criticisms of inefficiency and make-work in the construction and white-collar projects since they were designed to make work for as many people as possible. The principal response to these criticisms was therefore to expand production-for-use projects. The goal was to provide this kind of work for 15 percent of the people on the EWRP rolls—a target that was met by October 1934, when 15.3 percent of those on EWRP were working in production-for-use, up from only 5.4 percent the previous May.[18]

Three additional factors contributed to the focus on production-for-use. First, it was hoped that these projects would add to the efficiency of the entire set of New Deal programs by using more of the surplus commodities collected by the Agricultural Adjustment Administration (AAA) in its effort to raise the price of agricultural commodities by reducing their supply—thereby avoiding a repeat of the previous fall's outcry in response to the AAA's "destruction tactics" of plowing under cotton and slaughtering pigs. While the Federal Surplus Relief Corporation (FSRC) had been established the previous October to find use for some of these goods, primarily through distribution as in-kind relief, surpluses of such goods as cotton were still enormous. Second, production-for-use was the most important source of work relief for women and quickly provided work for two-thirds of all the women on the EWRP. Third, it was one of the least expensive types of project, since the materials were "free" (they came from the FSRC) and the blue-collar women on the projects received the lowest work-relief wage rates.[19]

The most common production-for-use projects were the labor-intensive sewing rooms, which were expanded from the early FERA and the CWA. Clothing remained the good most

Women at work at an integrated mattress-making project in Topeka, Kansas. [National Archives]

often produced, but other items, ranging from rag rugs to corn brooms, were made as well. Subsistence gardens were also expanded. In fact, state and local relief agencies were instructed to refuse relief to families on the Rural Rehabilitation Program if they had space for a home garden but failed to plant one. Community gardens were added to the list, and were complimented by projects to can or dry the garden produce. While subsistence gardens provided up to half of the production-for-use work during the summer months, they provided only 10 percent during the winter and spring.[20]

Projects to process animals dying from the drought were also expanded, as both existing facilities and emergency processing centers were used. More than 12 million cows, sheep, and goats were slaughtered and preserved in 1933 and 1934. While the FSRC purchased the animals for processing, the FERA oversaw the production and distribution of the canned goods.[21]

The sewing rooms, which had initially been set up in the 1800s, and the gardens and canning projects, which began under the FERA and CWA, were considered appropriate relief work by the business community. The same could not be said of the new production-for-use projects, however. These included a mattress-making project, projects to make clothing and other articles from the hides of drought-stricken cattle, and the Ohio Plan to put the unemployed to work in idle factories. (Businesspeople also complained about FERA aid to the self-help cooperatives, discussed in Chapter 2, which started soon after the FERA was set up.) Even though all of the goods produced were distributed only to others on relief or used in relief projects or in public institutions (e.g., hospitals)—nothing was sold through normal market channels—these projects were attacked vehemently for competing unfairly with the private sector.

The mattress-making project, which was planned during the winter of 1934 as a joint venture of the FERA and the AAA, expanded the work already being done in the sewing rooms in which some bedding (mostly comforters), as well as towels, pillow cases, sheets, and mattresses had been produced. Relief officials were especially anxious to find uses for some of the 2.5 million bales of cotton that had been taken off the market by the AAA, as well as to provide work relief for women and bedding for some of the people who desperately needed it.[22]

In June 1934 the FERA authorized the purchase of 250,000 bales of cotton (only one-tenth of the cotton surplus), along with ticking, sheeting, and toweling, for the production of 2 million mattresses, several million comforters, and other cotton products. It was clearly stipulated that these goods would remain outside normal market channels: they would only be distributed to relief recipients or used in other relief programs (primarily to provide bedding in the transient camps and shelters). By August, forty states, mostly in the South, had a total of 559 workrooms where women sewed mattresses and other bedding by hand, using frames built by men on relief.[23]

Another new set of projects was designed to use the hides, pelts, and wool that were byproducts of the animal-processing centers. Cowhides were tanned and used to repair shoes or made into goods, primarily wearing apparel and harnesses. Sheep wool was spun and woven, and then used for suits, coats, and other articles of clothing.[24]

Finally, there was the Ohio Plan, which was established in June 1934 with the incorporation of the Ohio Relief Production Units by the State Relief Commission of Ohio. These projects, which were known as the Ohio Plan even when they spread to other states, were designed to put people on relief to work in factories that had been partially or entirely shut down and then rented by state or local relief administrations. Ohio relief officials had great hopes for the plan, which they believed would provide work for all of the 56,000 unemployed industrial workers in Ohio, and in the summer of 1934 conducted a survey of all factories in the state to determine which ones could be used in the program. They began with twelve, producing clothing (suits, jackets, pants, shirts, dresses, and hosiery), furniture (primarily wooden beds and chairs), metalware (stoves, heaters, and skillets), china, and blankets—all in a variety of styles so that they would not be seen as "relief goods." The production was as close to a normal factory operation as possible. Wage rates were determined by the NRA code for the industry involved, and some variation was allowed in hours of work in order to fit into one of two workshifts. Skilled workers and supervisory personnel who were not on relief, often including the former manager of the plant, made up less than 10 percent of the workforce. Most of the workers were former employees—only they were now being paid by the EWRP.

In order to forestall protests from the business community, relief officials promised that there would be no competition with private industry. The goods produced were distributed only through relief channels to others on relief, thus remaining totally

A sign at a 1934 hunger march in Dallas, Texas, asks the president to take over idle factories. [AP/Wide World Photos]

outside the normal market. Business was further assured that workers would be asked to leave the work program if "real jobs" became available in private industry, and that the entire factory would reopen as a "normal enterprise" if it again became profitable to do so.[25] The Ohio Plan spread to other states. A long-underwear factory in Bay City, Michigan, that employed 250 people was reopened; enough underwear was produced "to provide every relief family in the state with two sets for the winter." Two additional underwear factories were reopened in Maine and at least two knitting mills were reopened in Massachusetts. As in Ohio, most of the workers had previously been employed in the factories.[26]

Relief officials believed that combining idle workers and idle factories was an eminently logical response to criticisms of earlier projects as make-work and inefficient. The work was efficient since it was carried out in factories with the latest equipment—in contrast to the "pick and shovel" construction projects. This also meant that it was seen by workers as "real work," a view that relief officials believed would help preserve people's "work skills," "work ethic," and morale in a way that previous programs had not. Finally, well-made goods were produced for needy families.[27]

In the summer of 1934 federal relief officials therefore developed plans to further increase the number of production-for-use projects. In June, relief official Lawrence Westbrook released a proposal to vastly expand the number of plants that would be used for canning meat, fish, fruit, and vegetables. North Carolina officials planned projects in which coal would be mined and agricultural lime would be quarried to produce fertilizer. In the District of Columbia, there were plans for an extensive Rehabilitation Corporation that would establish a system of cooperatives, including a sewing shop, a cannery, and a furniture factory, and would purchase or lease land in nearby Maryland or Virginia to grow food for relief processing and distribution. It was understood that if this proved successful it would be extended to other states. In addition, the FERA and the FSRC had plans to increase the production of shoes and other leather products from the hides of drought-stricken animals.[28]

Yet these plans never came to fruition. Production-for-use projects came up against the most fundamental contradiction of all FERA policies and projects: they challenged the logic of production-for-profit, and business and industry rose up in protest. The problem was that in production-for-use projects, goods were produced under the aegis of the government, which made its decisions on the basis of people's needs instead of business's profits. Thus it exposed the inability of the existing economic system to provide necessary goods as well as jobs. And it raised ominous fears of government taking over whole sectors of the economy, leading to the system most feared by profit-oriented capitalists—socialism. We turn to the attack on work relief projects in the next chapter.

5

THE ATTACK
ON WORK RELIEF

The year 1934 was one of flux. The recovery promised by the Roosevelt administration was not materializing: production remained stagnant and unemployment had fallen only slightly. Complaints about existing and evolving New Deal policies were growing louder. They came from all directions: from organizations and politicians such as Upton Sinclair and Huey Long to the left of Roosevelt, and from groups such as the American Liberty League and Father Coughlin's Silver Shirts to the right.

REACTIONS TO THE NEW DEAL

Relief and other New Deal policies had excited progressives across the country, many of whom wanted to carry these programs further. Progressive policies were advocated in political

Striking workers picketing outside an Aluminum Company of America (ALCOA) plant. [AP/Wide World Photos]

campaigns, by labor unions, and through organized groups among the elderly and the unemployed. Louisiana Senator Huey Long's Share-Our-Wealth movement, which proposed to tax the rich in order to give every family "a home, a car, and a radio," attracted followers throughout the nation. Long also supported a minimum wage, a shortened work week, and a vastly expanded public works program. It was clear he would pose a threat to Roosevelt in the 1936 presidential campaign—a threat that was eliminated by his assassination in 1935.[1]

In California, Upton Sinclair, originally known for his novel *The Jungle*, an exposé of the meat-processing industry, won the Democratic Party nomination for governor in 1934 on the strength of his EPIC (End Poverty in California) program. Centered around an extensive system of production and consumption cooperatives, the program included plans for acquiring idle farm land for agricultural workers and idle factories for the industrial unemployed (much like the Ohio Plan). Sinclair also called for stiffer income and inheritance taxes, a tax on idle land, and the payment of $50 per month to needy persons over sixty years old. As the November 1934 elections approached, Sinclair added even more progressive planks to his program: a heavy tax on all corporations valued at $100,000 or more and the establishment of a cooperative commonwealth of California. But Sinclair's proposals went too far for most Democratic Party leaders, and their lack of support, along with underhanded campaign tactics by his opponents, led to his defeat in the election.[2]

There was also nationwide support for a plan developed by Dr. Francis Townsend, a physician from Long Beach, California, to pay $200 a month, financed by a 2 percent sales tax, to every citizen over the age of sixty who retired from the labor force. The organization of the elderly that developed in support of this proposal was so strong that congressional representatives throughout the country pledged to vote for it, and social security was showcased in the Social Security Act.[3]

In addition to the political campaigns, there was an upsurge of working-class organization, often led by people from the Communist Party and other progressive organizations. The labor movement had been relatively quiet in the 1920s, as courts routinely issued injunctions forcing strikers to return to work and allowed employers to carry out a variety of anti-union actions (for example, forcing workers to sign "yellow-dog contracts" stating that they would never join a union). But strikes increased after the passage of the National Industrial Recovery Act in June 1933, which for the first time guaranteed the right of workers to organize unions of their own choosing and mandated that employers bargain in good faith with these unions.[4]

The promise of the NIRA, the despair of the ongoing depression, and the protests of other groups, primarily the unemployed and farmers, all contributed to an upsurge in union activity. As workers became more aware of their power, the strikes became increasingly militant and were often met with armed employer opposition and police violence. Four strikes in particular, in which entire cities were mobilized, were termed "social upheavals" by labor historian Irving Bernstein. Autoworkers in Toledo, Ohio, who were striking for increased wages, seniority, and union recognition, were joined on the picket lines by members of the local unemployed council. Together they fought police and National Guardsmen, forced management to bargain, and won most of their demands. A strike by longshoremen in San Francisco became a citywide general strike in the face of police violence. The strikers won their wage and hour demands, as well as the right to a union hiring hall. In Minneapolis, Minnesota, there was close to open class warfare as teamsters forced employers to bargain and raise wages. (The fourth "social upheaval," in the textile industry, will be discussed later in this chapter.)[5]

Many smaller strikes occurred as well, primarily for union recognition, higher wages, and better working conditions. Striking taxicab drivers in Philadelphia burned their cabs, and drivers in New York City took thousands of cabs off the streets. Copper miners in Butte, Montana, closed the Anaconda pits for several months. Farm workers in the lettuce fields in California's Salinas Valley and the tomato fields in southern New Jersey also went on strike. The large unions were energized in coal, and were organized for the first time in automobiles and steel.[6]

Strikes were not confined to the employed. CWA workers in New York City set a precedent when they went on strike in December 1933. FERA workers followed suit in the spring and summer of 1934, going on strike in Denver, Colorado, Dickson City, Pennsylvania, Meigs County, Ohio, Creedmore, Long Island, and Rochester, New York, to demand higher work-relief wage rates and to protest cuts in hours as well as unfair treatment of people who tried to organize on the projects. There were also hunger marches and other demonstrations to demand increased

The police attacking demonstrators outside a shantytown. [Culver Pictures, Inc.]

relief. Police frequently attacked the demonstrators: they killed two at a July protest at the Cleveland, Ohio, relief agency office, wounded fifty in a June demonstration at the Los Angeles, California, county welfare offices, hurt thirty at a September protest at FERA headquarters in Phoenix, Arizona, and injured twenty in an October march outside Albany, New York.[7]

There were other kinds of protest as well. In rural Arkansas the Southern Tenant Farmers' Union was formed in response to evictions caused by the AAA's crop reduction programs. Tenant farmers and sharecroppers, at least half of them black, called for cooperative agricultural communities to replace the southern plantation system. When the union grew to 10,000 members, the white power structure struck back, flogging, jailing, and murdering the organizers.[8]

As the momentum to expand the New Deal grew, the forces that opposed it grew increasingly vocal as well. The work programs were the focus of much of the controversy, and when, in June, Roosevelt appointed a Committee on Economic Security to develop a permanent system of relief, the criticism intensified.

Radio priest Father Coughlin became increasingly reactionary and anti-semitic, gathering support with his denunciations of bankers and theories of financial conspiracy. With a weekly audience estimated at between 30 and 45 million, he received more mail than anyone else in the country, including the President. In November 1934, he formed the National Union for Social Justice, whose fascist Silver Shirts served as a frightening reminder of the Nazis in Europe.[9]

From the beginning, business opposition to the New Deal had been expressed through the Chamber of Commerce and the National Association of Manufacturers. Representatives from these groups rarely failed to testify at congressional hearings or to publish counterproposals to New Deal policies. But by 1934, the industrial giants believed that this was not sufficient, and in August 1934 they organized the American Liberty League. Dominated by such huge corporations as DuPont and General Motors, the League campaigned against what it saw as a developing welfare state that was encroaching on their territory. According to Roosevelt historian Arthur Schlesinger, Wall Street saw the American Liberty League as "little short of an answer to a prayer."[10]

THE DEBATE OVER THE WORK PROGRAMS

The work programs were one of the League's primary targets. Reiterating complaints that high relief wage rates were leading to labor shortages, that the projects were only boondoggles and make-work, that the work was done inefficiently, that the programs competed unfairly with the private sector, and that the entire enterprise was too expensive and was prone to graft and corruption, they called for an end to all federally supported work relief and the resumption of local responsibility for the unemployed. In other words, the federal government should do little or nothing, as it had before the New Deal.[11]

The League's views were clearly articulated by the Joint Business Conference for Economic Recovery, held in December 1934. The Conference Report, which was entered into the *Congressional Digest*, complained that the government was forcing up wage rates by paying relief workers too much, thereby creating labor shortages, especially of low-wage labor, and that it was competing unfairly by producing goods that the private sector also produced. In sum, relief projects were impeding the return of business confidence, increasing unemployment, and undermining the recovery.

The Joint Business Conference for Economic Recovery had its own recommendations. In place of the massive, innovative work programs, they advocated that direct relief should be used in place of work relief whenever possible, all work relief should be in the form of construction projects, people should be paid no more than they would receive for direct relief, and all relief should be reduced in order to balance the federal budget. They argued further that this was the only way to end the Depression:

> The most effective solution of the problem of unemployment and relief is the creation of such confidence between industry and the government that business can proceed with plans to develop new industries, to enlarge existing enterprises, and freely to place private capital in the investment field.[12]

Although the most common objections were that the work relief programs were too expensive or were boondoggles in which people were paid far too much for inefficient and unnecessary make-work, the fundamental issue was the fear that the programs were interfering with the private sector's ability to make a profit. Thus the attack on the production-for-use projects was particularly virulent. While only a few months earlier, when the CWA ended, production-for-use had been seen as the most logical response to criticisms of make-work, during the following fall the

A woman preparing beans, which have been grown in a gardening
project, for canning. [National Archives]

projects were seriously restricted. Nels Anderson, director of
labor relations in the WPA, described this Catch-22 situation: "If
a project is useful it is sure to be criticized because it is competitive, while if it is non-competitive it is just as likely to be con-
demned by the same critics as not being useful."[13]

Arguing vigorously against production-for-use, the business
community claimed that the goods produced competed unfairly
with the private sector, taking away from sales of their products—
even though the goods were distributed only to people on relief
who had minimal resources after five years of depression. As J.C.
Lindsey, a regional engineer for FERA, explained in response to
complaints that FERA shoe repair shops would take business
away from private merchants, "If these shoes were not repaired

or furnished by us, the men and women for whom we are doing this work would simply be without shoes."[14]

The underlying problem was that production-for-use projects raised a critical question: since production-for-profit was not a sufficient motive to induce business to produce needed goods and the government was producing them instead, why depend on the private sector at all? This sentiment was further reflected in the Joint Business Conference Report, which ominously predicted that "Government competition with private business leads toward socialism."[15] But this was simply the business sector's worst fear: that the system of production-for-profit would be replaced by production-for-use. As *Business Week* explained, capitalists were not really worried about competition from the existing small scale of production-for-use, but were concerned instead about "the uncomfortable thought that government manufacture might be expanded widely and might become permanent."[16]

Relief officials defended the work programs. They hoped that the higher wage rates would help spark economic recovery by increasing the purchasing power of large numbers of people. Some maintained, apologetically, that they were doing as well as possible given their constraints, and claimed that the problems stemmed from the programs' contradictory purposes, as both work programs and relief programs. As a work program, people were supposed to perform useful work in an efficient manner. But as a relief program, as many of the needy as possible were supposed to be given aid. Furthermore, those considered most in need were to be given preference, while their ability was of secondary importance, leading to the practice of bypassing younger, and often stronger, workers, in favor of the head of the household.

Taking another line of reasoning, some relief officials argued that efficiency and other business criteria were simply not appropriate for evaluating work programs. Nels Anderson declared that the government had different goals than private industry as it was "guided by social rather than profit motivations."[17] He explained further: "[W]ithout denying the validity of the profit test for private industry, we can still deny that the same test need be applied to all workers on public projects."[18] And Harry Hopkins, chief administrator of all three programs, argued:

> In the relief business where our raw material is misery and our finished product nothing more than amelioration, effectiveness has to be measured in less ambitious terms than success. That word applies better to marginal profit, cash or otherwise. Relief deals with human insolvency.[19]

But business sector criticisms were considered too strong to ignore, and throughout the fall of 1934 the scope of the work programs was considerably narrowed.

REFORM AND REACTION IN THE FALL OF 1934

By the fall of 1934 it had become clear that the New Deal programs were not substantially increasing either production or employment. Industrial production fell 15 percent from late June through late August, and unemployment hovered at approximately 22 percent of the total labor force—and 33 percent of the industrial labor force.[20] But while the fall of 1933 saw the development of the massive CWA, the fall of 1934 was a time of retrenchment.

Hopkins began the process in early September with the announcement that the entire relief program would be tightened during the upcoming winter. The federal government would make sure that the states paid their fair share of relief, and all families on the FERA would be rechecked to make sure that only the needy received relief.[21] But this was only the appetizer for the main course that followed. Four major changes in FERA policy were announced, all of which were aimed at reducing the effect that relief payments had on low-wage labor markets and at making the program conform more closely to the logic of production-for-profit.

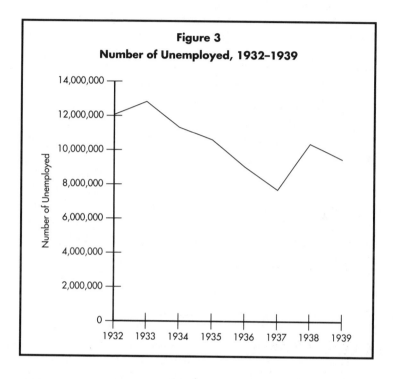

Figure 3
Number of Unemployed, 1932–1939

Ending Direct Relief for Strikers

The first change was to end all direct relief for strikers. Initial FERA policy regarding such relief had been established in October 1933 and authorized local relief agencies to provide relief to workers on strike unless the National Labor Board (established through the NIRA) ruled that the basis of the strike was unreasonable and unjustified.[22] Not surprisingly, the business community charged that this policy was tantamount to the federal government underwriting strikes, since it allowed strikers to hold out longer than would have been possible otherwise. The Illinois Manufacturers' Association, a vocal opponent of many New Deal policies, insisted that giving relief to strikers was an invitation to "industrial warfare and strife." Others argued that taxpayer money should not be used to support people who were "voluntarily unemployed." In response to this type of criticism, some local relief administrations began to deny relief to strikers in their areas. As Syracuse, New York, Mayor Roland B. Marvin explained when strikers were removed from his city's relief rolls in May, "That is one way of starving workers into accepting any terms of employment offered them."[23]

The controversy came to a head during the textile strike in the fall of 1934. In an industry characterized by low wages and oppressive working conditions, the strike caught fire, quickly spreading through the eastern states from Maine to Alabama. By mid-September, more than 400,000 workers were out on strike, and criticisms of FERA policy grew more intense. Relief administrators in Maine, New Jersey, and Alabama followed the example set in Syracuse, disobeying FERA regulations and terminating aid for the strikers. Officials in Waterville, Maine, explained their reasoning: "Let the unions support them. They'll either work or not eat. Anyone who strikes in these times deserves to starve." In North Carolina, South Carolina, and Georgia, people were taken off relief if they simply had a close relative on strike.[24]

On September 13, FERA administrators reaffirmed that striking workers were entitled to receive relief. However, within days they ruled that able-bodied workers had to work if they were to receive relief payments. This would have meant going on work relief, and therefore leaving the picket line or other strike activities. However, this was not considered sufficient, and the next day FERA rescinded the original policy and ruled that the decision about whether or not to give relief to strikers would be left up to the states. In other words, state and local relief administrations were given official permission by federal relief officials to do what they were already doing—denying relief to strikers.[25]

Striking textile workers marching through Gastonia, North Carolina. [AP/Wide World Photos]

Wage-Rate Policies: Removing Workers from Relief Rolls and Ending the Minimum Rate

Work relief wage-rate policies had been a source of heated debate since the FERA began. Although the minimum was reduced from $.40 to $.30 when the CWA ended in March 1934, this was not enough for agricultural employers throughout the country and for most white Southerners, who remained steadfast in their bitter objections to the $.30 per hour minimum. Their concerns were understandable, especially in the rural South where private sector wages were often as low as $.10 to $.125 cents per hour, making $.30 an hour seem very attractive. Southerners were particularly upset that African-Americans were receiving relief since it gave them an alternative to low-wage private sector jobs.

By the fall of 1934 some state and local relief officials responded to these protests by resuming the pre-FERA practice of suspending relief when additional workers were needed, especially in agriculture.[26] Not surprisingly, this was most common in cotton and tobacco regions, as these crops depended on large supplies of labor, especially of African-Americans in the southeast and Mexican-Americans in the southwest. What agricultural employers wanted was to have many more people available for work than they could employ, a group that would therefore be so desperate for work that they would accept very low wages. This is exactly what happened when relief was cut back. As Thad Holt, director of the Alabama Relief Administration, wrote to Harry Hopkins in September 1934, at least 9,000 day laborers had been dropped from the Alabama relief rolls, many of whom would not be able to find work, and consequently "anybody applying for cotton-pickers can have ten of them for the job."[27]

Instead of forbidding these cuts, FERA officials allowed them. As a directive issued on September 21, 1934, stated, "The Federal Emergency Relief Administration not only approves this procedure, but insists upon its being followed by those States in which conditions of seasonal employment warrant such action." Furthermore, in order to help insure that this would happen, FERA administrators cut federal aid to states in which cotton and tobacco were grown. Insisting that able-bodied people on the rolls should obtain agricultural work, they would be "requiring new and conclusive proof of inability to get a job before resuming aid." [28]

While the new FERA policy of closing the rolls during planting and harvesting was welcomed by agricultural employers, they were still opposed to the $.30 per hour minimum. They were joined by others who complained that they could not find domestic service workers, primarily African-American women, who were receiving relief instead. Caving in to this pressure, FERA officials issued a directive on November 19 that stated simply,

... all previous rules and regulations governing minimum hourly rates of pay are herewith rescinded so that the prevailing rate in the community for the kind of work performed will be the governing factor in determining hourly wage rates hereafter.[29]

Federal relief administrator Edward A. Williams explained that strong opposition to the $.30 per hour minimum had finally led the FERA to abandon it. The *New York Times* explained simply that the FERA had "capitulated."[30]

The ruling had the desired effect, and by January 1935 work relief rates had plummeted throughout the South. In Alabama, Georgia, South Carolina, and Tennessee, rates between $.10 and $.20 per hour predominated, and in rural areas throughout the rest of the South rates fell to between $.10 and $.12 per hour. Apparently anticipating these results, in some southern states relief officials urged local agencies to prevent work relief wage rates from falling below $.10 per hour.[31]

Ending the Controversial Production-for-Use Projects

Production-for-use projects were also cut that fall. As the projects had been expanded during the spring and summer of 1934, and as new proposals were unveiled, the business community grew apoplectic. The situation was described in *The Nation*:

[The FSRC] and the FERA operate in an atmosphere of continuous protest and conflict. Practically everything they do or try to do is violently denounced by the vested interests of private business, which see these government agencies moving steadily, and in response to overwhelming pressures, toward the taking over of whole sectors of the process of production and distribution which have hitherto been the province of profit-motivated business-as-usual.[32]

Unlike most of the other contentious relief issues, however, little of the struggle over production-for-use was carried out in the open. As *Business Week* noted, the FERA tried to "soft-pedal the whole business."[33] Nevertheless, the complaints evoked responses. As Joanna Colcord wrote in a report for *The Survey,* "Each trial balloon sent up from Washington in relation to governmental production-for-use has been promptly shot down in enraged sorties by manufacturers."[34]

Thus in response to complaints about work relief in coal mines, from both mine owners, who wanted to protect their markets, and the United Mine Workers, which wanted to protect their jobs, FERA officials announced that there would no federal fuel plan for winter of 1934-1935. Unlike the previous winter, when the federal administration took responsibility for assuring that the people on relief received fuel, this would now be left up to the states. Federal relief officials also announced that a small admission fee could be charged to arts exhibits and performances for those who could pay, and reminded state and local agencies that these must not compete with non-relief facilities.[35]

Federal aid to self-help cooperatives was also severely cut in response to a "great protest" from industry whenever a government agency purchased goods produced by a cooperative. In addition to procuring less cooperative output, FERA aid was also reduced outright. Thus cooperatives in California, where most were located, received less than one-half of 1 percent of total FERA funds between January 1933 and June 1935.[36]

The mattress-making project had elicited "howls of protest from mattress manufacturers."[37] It was also criticized by manufacturers of other goods who "were afraid of what mattress-making might lead to."[38] As a result, it was cut back less than three months after it was established: the original plan to produce 2 million mattresses was reduced to only 1 million.[39]

Similarly, the projects for processing animals dying from the drought were criticized by retailers of processed foods, especially meat, as were the projects for processing animals hides, pelts, and wool. These protests intensified during the late summer of 1934 as proposals were released to increase the production of shoes and other leather products. Again, FERA officials acceded to these complaints, announcing that instead of using the approxi-

The PWA built massive structures such as the Triborough Bridge but was not at first allowed to build housing. [National Archives]

mately 3.5 million hides already in storage for work-relief projects, they would be sold for processing in the private sector.[40]

But it was the Ohio Plan that was the most contentious of all the production-for-use projects. Although it had received strong support from relief administrators, relief workers, and those industrialists whose factories were rented, this support was not nearly enough to stem the tidal wave of objections. The attack was so effective that by March 1935, the Ohio Plan had been completely dismantled. As *Business Week* put it: "So far as FERA is concerned, it is apparent now that it will not fly in the face of the indignant protest of business by countenancing any extensive excursion into the field of private industry."[41]

Cuts in Other Employment Programs

The dismantling of relief projects and the restrictions on relief policies were mirrored in other New Deal programs. It was announced that there would be no further projects like the TVA, which had begun operating in October 1934 and immediately proved to be a successful example of public production: the price of electricity in the area it served had fallen quickly and it was expected that within ten years the program would become self-liquidating. Yet its very success doomed other such projects. The *Wall Street Journal* expressed the opposition of private contractors: "That is the potential, if not actual, destruction of capital."[42]

Similarly, the PWA plan to construct several thousand units of low-rent housing was never carried out. Congress had allocated $125 million for this program, which was designed to provide decent housing for some of the estimated 1.5 million people who lived in inadequate quarters, as well as to create jobs for construction workers in the severely depressed building trades industry.[43] However, the project was torpedoed by strong opposition from private contractors and other business interests. Joseph P. Day, an auctioneer and broker, expressed their views when he argued that "a much more logical method of supplying new suites would be to have public money loaned to private builders, who would rent the building for what they could get."[44] Instead of extensive low-rent housing built through the PWA, private contractors got their way in the Federal Housing Authority (FHA), which insured loans made by private lending institutions to individuals to buy new homes or repair existing ones. As explained in the *Congressional Digest*, the "principal aim of the [FHA] was to make home financing, on reasonable terms to the borrower, safe and attractive to private capital."[45]

At the same time that FERA policies were being dismantled, federal officials were developing plans for what would become the Works Progress Administration and the Social Security Act, both of which were profoundly affected by the struggles described above. We turn to this in the next chapter.

6

THE SOCIAL SECURITY ACT AND THE WPA: THE RESPONSE TO THE CONSERVATIVE ATTACK

The attack on the work programs was effective. Not only did it constrain the EWRP, but it also limited the Social Security Act and the Works Progress Administration (WPA), which were developed from the summer of 1934 through the following summer of 1935. While the Social Security Act provided the foundation for a permanent program of direct relief, the work program continued on a temporary, emergency basis in the WPA. And state and local relief authorities were again given responsibility for people considered "unemployable," whose situation became especially desperate.

THE SOCIAL SECURITY ACT

Work on the Social Security Act began with Roosevelt's appointment of the Committee on Economic Security in June 1934. Subcommittees were quickly established to design programs for unemployment compensation, old-age insurance (social security), supplementary (categorical) assistance, medical care, and public employment. However, Roosevelt's original vision of "cradle to grave" security for all Americans became increasingly constricted. The American Medical Association's opposition to any type of national health care was so strong that a medical care program was never even formulated.[1] And a voluntary work program similar to the FERA and CWA was missing as well. The final act included only three types of programs: social insurance programs, i.e., social security and unemployment compensation; categorical assistance programs, i.e., Old Age Assistance (OAA) for those failing to qualify for social security, Aid to Dependent Children (ADC), and Aid to the Blind (AB); and limited funds for public health. As relief analyst Maxwell Stewart wrote of the final act, "Hailed as the most progressive social measure in this generation, it is in some respects thoroughly reactionary."[2]

Other aspects of the Social Security Act also contributed to its conservative nature. First, although there was a good deal of support for financing the social insurance programs from potentially progressive income taxes, as most Western European countries did, the money was to come from payroll taxes. Second, gender and racial discrimination were embedded in these programs, which were designed as income replacement for lost wages primarily for white men, while most women and people of color were to receive aid through the socially stigmatized categorical assistance programs. Further clarifying this distinction, those who worked in agriculture, domestic service, the government, and nonprofit organizations—jobs typically held by white women and people of color—were specifically excluded from social insurance.

Third, racial discrimination was also apparent in the Old Age

Evicted sharecroppers line the road in New Madrid County, Missouri. [Library of Congress]

Assistance program. While the draft version mandated that it provide "a reasonable subsistence compatible with decency and health" and that aid could not be denied if requirements of age and need were met, in the final act these were replaced by the virtually meaningless phrase that payments would be furnished "as far as practicable under the conditions in each State." University of Chicago economist Paul H. Douglas explained that the original phrase had been deleted because southern Congressmen feared that it "might be used by authorities in Washington to compel the southern states to pay higher pensions to aged Negroes than the dominant white groups believed to be desirable."[3]

Fourth, the amounts that would be given for all of the categorical assistance programs were extremely low, and many decisions about both categorical assistance and unemployment compensation were left to the discretion of individual states. Conservative "states' rights" advocates got their way, and lower wage states were allowed to set correspondingly low levels of relief and to implement more restrictive regulations for unemployment compensation.

THE EXCLUSION OF EMPLOYMENT ASSURANCE

The initial version of the Social Security Act, entitled the Economic Security Act to reflect its more comprehensive scope, included a call for Employment Assurance. This would have provided public employment to anyone whose unemployment compensation had been exhausted, as well as to "able-bodied workers" not covered by unemployment compensation. As the Committee on Economic Security explained in its final report:

> While it will not always be necessary to have public-employment projects to give employment assurance, it should be recognized as a permanent policy of the Government and not merely as an emergency measure.[4]

There was a good deal of support for including a work program as part of a permanent federal relief system. Progressives involved in relief policy favored a "permanent system in which public works, unemployment insurance, and relief [would] all be soundly integrated."[5] However, they cautioned that work relief and direct relief should be separated in different measures since "mixing of work and [direct] relief is likely to deteriorate into forced labor" of the work-test.[6]

More mainstream groups also advocated a permanent federal work program, understood to focus on white men, that would be separate from direct relief. The International City Managers' Association endorsed such a program, which would be expanded to provide work for all "employables" on relief. And the U.S. Conference of Mayors championed a "permanent unemployment work-relief fund and program" that would include all types of workers, pay prevailing wage rates, and be administered by the federal government.[7]

FERA administrators also favored a permanent program of work relief, separate from the cash programs in the Social Security Act. Hopkins wrote that "any insurance plan would have to have with it a permanent public works program, to provide greater compensation against the hazards of unemployment."[8] According to historians Arthur W. Macmahon, John D. Millett, and Gladys Ogden, federal relief officials favored the separation of work relief and cash relief because of a "vague sort of institutional rivalry" between the Committee on Economic Security and the FERA, with FERA officials fearing that their power might be usurped if the work relief program was incorporated into an all-inclusive Social Security Act.[9]

Hopkins' plan was unveiled in November when he proposed a Federal Work Relief Corporation that would implement Employment Assurance as a separate work program. Hopkins described this as a sort of "permanent CWA," and proposed to spend between $8 billion and $9 billion over a two year period to create work for all of the employable jobless. Capturing the business sector's startled reaction, the New York Times dubbed the program EPIA—End Poverty in America—an extension of Upton Sinclair's EPIC program, which most people believed had been buried along with Sinclair's defeat that November and which the Times claimed could "safely be credited with spoiling the Thanksgiving Day dinners of many conservatives."[10]

But the battles over the FERA and CWA took their toll. Conservatives in the New Deal administration, who generally reflected the views of the business community, argued successfully against any type of permanent work program. Roosevelt's financial advisers, in particular, "threw their weight against a form of action that might have seemed to associate work relief efforts with the enactment of the beginnings of a permanent structure of security," since they "preferred to advance the works program as a strictly temporary expedient."[11] Instead of establishing a work

A shantytown in what is now Riverside Park on the Hudson River in New York City. [Culver Pictures, Inc.]

program as part of the Social Security Act itself or as a separate permanent program, public employment was relegated to the Works Progress Administration, another temporary program designed to meet the emergency needs created by the Depression.

ENDING DIRECT RELIEF FOR "UNEMPLOYABLES"

While people considered "unemployable" had received direct relief under the FERA, the federal government relinquished its responsibility for their care as the earlier program was replaced by the WPA in the fall of 1935. The political unpopularity of direct relief, as well as the inclusion of categorical assistance in the Social Security Act, allowed federal relief administrators, including Hopkins, to withdraw their support for federal direct relief and concentrate instead on work relief. Thus, as conservatives had demanded since the FERA began, "unemployables" were returned to the auspices of the state and local governments.[12]

Direct relief was ended gradually, first in the Southern states during the summer of 1935 and then throughout the rest of the country, so that by January 1936 federal aid for direct relief had been entirely handed back to the states. The same was true for transients: as estimates of their numbers decreased, responsibility for their care was also returned to the states. It quickly became clear that the state and local governments were unable to cope with this burden of direct relief, and both the numbers on the rolls and the amount each family received dropped sharply. Between June and December 1935, average monthly grants per case fell from $23 to $11 in Wisconsin, from $15 to $6 in South Dakota, and from $13 to $3 in North Carolina. In addition, a large proportion of relief was provided in kind, and in some areas of the country grocery orders and surplus commodities became the only source of aid.[13]

Relief practices designed to humiliate recipients were frequently resumed, which deterred otherwise eligible people from applying for aid. These included requiring pauper's oaths, having police and firemen investigate cases, forcing people to stand in line in public places in order to receive surplus commodities, and sending single people to almshouses and county poorhouses instead of providing relief in the community. And, although exceptions were sometimes made in cases involving young children, direct relief was rarely given to "employables" who were eligible for other forms of aid but were waiting for an assignment to the work program. Not surprisingly, transients seldom received anything.[14]

In addition, many local relief administrations brought back the work-test. Called "work-or-starve" by some commentators, these tests were established in spite of the fact that people considered "unemployable" were required to perform some type of labor in order to receive relief. While the use of work-tests varied from state to state, ranging from less than 2 percent of the families on direct relief in Virginia to over 25 percent in Kansas, by 1940 approximately 180,000 people in twenty-four states were subjected to the work-test and it had been authorized in nine more.[15]

As a result of these cuts in direct relief, unemployment again became more visible. Soup lines were set up, some states established "border patrols" to keep out unemployed people from other states, shantytowns of the homeless flourished once again, and begging was resumed in some areas. Despite this, the federal government stuck to the policy of local responsibility for "unemployables."[16]

THE WORKS PROGRESS ADMINISTRATION

The Works Progress Administration (WPA) was signed into law on April 8, 1935. Because it was designed as a temporary measure, Congressional reauthorization was required each year, which made it difficult to know ahead of time how much money would be allocated and therefore to develop effective long-term plans. The rolls fluctuated widely. After an initial expansion to over 3 million people in early 1936, the program was cut back. But the sharp recession, which lasted from September 1937 through May 1938, caused the numbers to climb back up, to a high of 3.3 million by November 1938. Thereafter the program began a steady decline, and there were only 42,000 people on the rolls when it closed on June 30, 1943.

Wage-Rate and Hour Policies

The WPA maintained the means-test as the key to determining eligibility.[17] However, in order to make work on the program seem more like a "real job" and less like the "dole," relief administrators abandoned the FERA's budgetary deficiency method of determining a family's monthly payment. Instead they used a

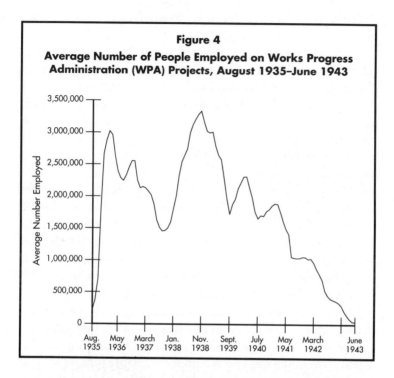

Figure 4

Average Number of People Employed on Works Progress Administration (WPA) Projects, August 1935–June 1943

scale based on three factors: the region of the country in which a person lived, the degree of urbanization of the community, and the individual's skill level. The initial result was a list of eighty different payments, ranging from $19 per month—less than $1 per day, and far below the old $.30 cents per hour minimum—to $94 per month.[18]

The main debate was over how many hours a person could work: should it be a fixed number, the same for everyone, and therefore not based on private sector wage rates for similar work; or should the hours be calculated by dividing the total payment by the prevailing wage rate for each type of labor. The latter was strongly supported by organized labor, which believed that it would help maintain private sector wage rates, particularly for skilled workers, by clearly tying work-relief rates to labor market rates.[19]

When the WPA began, payments were based on what was called a "security wage." This meant that workers were paid even if time on the project was lost due to weather conditions or other factors beyond their control. Prevailing wage rates were not used, and the number of hours people could work ranged from 120 to 140 per month. However, in 1936, a year after the program started, the policy was modified. While the total payment was still determined by the security wage, it was now divided by the prevailing local wage rate in the area for each type of work in order to determine the number of hours a person could work. This led to many different payment schedules. In New York City, for instance, the combination of different monthly payments divided by prevailing wage rates led to 125 different schedules, and throughout the country the combinations of different monthly payments and hourly rates led to 4,000 schedules.[20]

Finally, in August 1939, the prevailing wage policy was abandoned. Arguing that the many schedules resulting from different people working different numbers of hours was leading to inefficiency, the hours were set at a uniform 130 per month. Federal relief officials, anticipating protests from organized labor, instituted the policy quickly. Despite sit-down strikes held on several projects and a 14 percent decrease in the average hourly work-relief wage rate, the prevailing wage policy was not brought back.[21]

Through all these changes, average payments on the WPA remained below private sector wages. As a result, WPA payments remained too low to meet people's needs, especially those in large families, and often had to be supplemented from other sources. Direct relief, federal surplus commodities, and wages from private employment provided additional income for the families of many WPA workers. Although little data exists on the extent of this practice, a March 1936 survey of relief in thirteen cities found that in the WPA, as in the FERA, approximately 25 percent of all workers received additional income and/or surplus commodities.[22]

WPA workers in a recreational education project in Pennsylvania demanding better pay. [AP/Wide World Photos]

Fear of competition with the private sector was at the basis of many WPA policies—a legacy of the battles of the previous years—and WPA workers were required to accept private sector employment if it became available. In the beginning, this requirement held even if the private sector wages were lower than the hourly rate a person could earn on the WPA. In 1937 this policy was changed in response to pressure from organized labor, and WPA workers were required to take private sector jobs only if the wages were greater than or equal to the amount that could be earned on the work program. But after two years of complaints, WPA administrators returned to the initial policy of requiring individuals to accept private sector employment at any rate of pay.[23]

Another policy change in 1939 was designed to reduce competition with the private sector even further. The "18-month provision" mandated that people who had been working on a WPA project for eighteen continuous months had to be removed from the rolls and wait thirty days before they could be reassigned to another project. Since there were always more workers waiting for assignments than there were available placements, people often had to wait many months before again obtaining WPA work. In conjunction with the requirement that WPA workers accept any private sector job, even if the pay was less than the amount they made on the WPA, this also pushed relief workers into low-wage jobs.[24]

Increased desperation did not create jobs, however. A survey of almost one-fifth of the nearly 783,000 people who were removed from the WPA rolls in July and August 1939 (when the "18-month provision" was implemented) found that by the following February only 13 percent had found employment; over half of the dismissed workers were back on the WPA, while many others had turned to direct relief.[25]

Discrimination Continues

Wage differentials based on gender, race, and class were again carried over from the rest of the economy to the WPA, as they had been in both FERA and the CWA. From the inception of the WPA through June 1942, those on building projects, primarily skilled Caucasian craftsmen, as well as those on white-collar service projects, were paid an average of $.57 per hour. In contrast, blue-collar women on sewing and other goods-production projects, as well as the primarily unskilled and often African-American men on sanitation projects, received an average of only $.39 per hour, and the millions of unskilled (black and white) men who worked on the road projects were paid an average of $.43 per hour.[26]

In spite of ongoing criticism, FERA policies toward women and African-Americans showed little improvement under the

WPA. New Deal officials had always been concerned about the need to maintain the "traditional family"—husband, wife, and children—and so, despite their increased unemployment and increased need, women were subjected to the same forms of discrimination that had pervaded the FERA and the CWA. If at all possible, men were considered the "economic head" of the family and were therefore the first to be put on the rolls. This was clearly spelled out in the Louisiana WPA manual: "As a general rule, a woman with an employable husband is not eligible for referral, as her husband is the logical head of the family."[27] According to historian Donald S. Howard, the husband's position had to be protected even if this involved putting "some brake upon women's eagerness to be the family breadwinner, wage recipient, and controller of the family pocketbook."[28] By the late 1930s this concern had also led to abandoning the earlier practice of bypassing the husband in favor of a younger worker. Although younger workers were seen as more productive, it was believed that choosing them instead of their fathers would "weaken the responsibility and authority of the family head and injure the family structure."[29]

In addition to trying to preserve men's authority in families, WPA administrators wanted to "protect the WPA program against possible public criticisms for employing 'too many women.'"[30] Thus while women comprised almost 25 percent of the labor force, they were kept to only one-sixth of the total WPA rolls. As a result, in 1936 Hopkins ordered the Colorado WPA to remove almost half of the women from its program—it had been discovered that they comprised 27 percent of the Colorado rolls, compared to 16 percent nationally.[31]

Like women, African-Americans continued to suffer discrimination in the WPA. This was ensured by a variety of blatant practices, most of which were carried over from the earlier work programs. The number of blacks on the rolls was sometimes restricted to a specified proportion of the total and they were routinely forced off the program entirely when their labor was

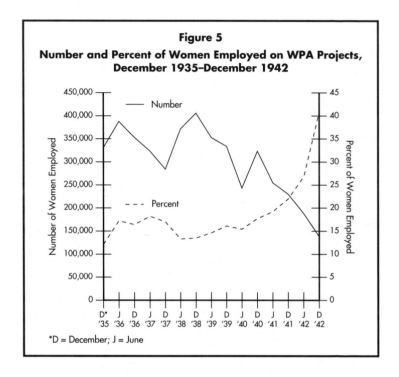

Figure 5

Number and Percent of Women Employed on WPA Projects, December 1935–December 1942

*D = December; J = June

needed in agriculture or in domestic service. When general re-
ductions were ordered, African-Americans were often dismissed
before whites.[32]

Total monthly payments to African-American and Mexi-
can-American women were sometimes limited by allowing
them to work only a portion of the usual amount of hours.
African-Americans were still considered to be "accustomed"
to lower wages and were therefore required to accept lower
paying jobs than whites; they could be denied WPA placements
if they failed to do so. They were still generally classified as
unskilled labor no matter what their actual skill levels. And
their applications were handled more slowly than those of
whites. Finally, there were still difficulties finding sponsors for

projects which included blacks and most of the projects remained segregated.[33]

Some small gains were made in the WPA for African-American white-collar workers. A few were put to work conducting research, in public health projects, and on the Federal Arts project. In addition, the segregated projects for blacks were now generally supervised by other African-Americans, and a few blacks were given administrative jobs in the relief program.[34]

But the gains were limited. Giving in to racist attitudes, African-Americans were not given positions on survey projects because "whites [did] not like to be interviewed by Negroes."[35] Relief agencies also went along with these practices, restricting the numbers of black caseworkers. The marginalization of African-Americans, and black women in particular, is evident in the statistics from the week ending April 2, 1938, when for the first time data was gathered on work program participation by gender and race. During that week African-American women comprised only 2.1 percent of the WPA rolls, black men comprised 12.1 percent, white women 11 percent, and white men 74.4 percent.[36]

The policy of removing whole groups of workers from the rolls when their labor was needed in the private sector, especially in domestic service and agriculture, was continued, and, as in the FERA, it disproportionately affected African-American women. As a result, even though women working in domestic service usually earned less than half of what they earned on the WPA, they were often forced off the rolls and "frankly told they must accept proffered employment [in domestic service] or be stricken forever from all relief rolls."[37] The Birmingham News, for example, reported that 150 black women were dropped from the WPA rolls in January 1937 "because of sharply increased demand for servants."[38] And a North Carolina relief official unapologetically described work program policy:

In April, 1936, all sewing rooms, both white and colored, in the strawberry section of this county were closed because of the fact that labor was available to these women both in picking and packing of strawberries. Since employment was available in the tobacco fields, these rooms were not re-opened until after the tobacco season, which was sometime during the month of November, 1936.[39]

The report continued:

Since the colored case load was so low in the county and business conditions in general were much improved, it was felt both by WPA authorities and also by local sponsors and the Department of Public Welfare that to re-open the colored sewing rooms would tend to increase the shortage of domestic labor in this county.[40]

A woman from Brewton, Alabama, wrote about the effect of her 1937 dismissal from the WPA:

They cut me off [the WPA rolls] and I have nothing to go upon. When they cut me off the first time they sent me to the blueberry farm and promise to put me back after the berries was over. But they didn't they told me to go to the cotton patch for 60 cents a hundred. And I really cant support myself and little girl at that rates for it is school time now and she hasnt got her books nor clothes.[41]

Projects

The content of WPA projects reflected lessons learned in the FERA and the CWA. Thus construction comprised the bulk of the work, absorbing 77 percent of the money spent.[44] While criticisms of inefficiency and boondoggles never stopped, and some of the recreational facilities, especially golf courses and ski runs, continued to come under fire as "public luxury improvements," construction had become a well-accepted form of work relief.

More than 650,000 miles of roads were constructed or repaired, along with bridges and viaducts, drainage ditches, culverts, sidewalks, curbs, gutters, traffic lighting and signs, and roadside landscaping. More than 125,000 buildings were built or repaired, almost one-third of which were schools. Others included libraries, auditoriums, gymnasiums, offices, hospitals,

WPA workers in Lawrence County, Tennessee, building a farm-to-market road. [National Archives]

penal institutions, dormitories, firehouses, garages, storage facilities, armories, and barns and stables. Almost 3,000 public utility plants were built and another 1,000 upgraded, and telephone and telegraph lines, electric power lines, water mains, water wells, and water storage tanks were installed. More than 2,100 swimming and wading pools were built or improved. Work on other outdoor recreational facilities included parks, playgrounds, stadiums, grandstands, bleachers, fairgrounds and rodeo grounds, athletic fields, tennis courts, golf courses, ice skating areas, ski runs and jumps, and bandshells. Other projects included flood and erosion control, monuments and historic markers, fencing, tunnels, docks, wharfs, and piers.[43]

Although manual labor was not considered suitable for white

**WPA arts projects: artists at work on a mural [National Archives];
the billboard and the leading character for a Federal Theater Project
production, written by Edwin Denby and Orson Welles; a sculptor
teaching a class in Harlem [Culver Pictures, Inc.].**

women, this constraint did not always apply to African-Americans. In 1936 some African-American women were put on "beautification" projects, laboring in groups and using picks and shovels to clean up roads and parks. This quickly elicited a stream of protest for giving such "gang labor" to African-American women, but not white women, and the projects were quickly cut.[44]

Projects for professional and nonmanual workers continued to come under fire as make-work, but they nevertheless took almost 11 percent of total WPA funds. They included research and records projects on a variety of economic and social topics (e.g., housing facilities, health surveys, studies of the effects of automation), as well as public records projects (e.g., indexing deeds and mortgages, mapping, and codifying municipal ordinances), historical records surveys (preserving records of historical importance), and research assistance in universities. The other major white-collar component of the program, which was called "public activities," included the education projects carried over from the FERA, as well as operating recreation programs, working in libraries and museums, and the Federal Arts Project, which set up music, art, writing, and theater projects. Artists created paintings, sculptures, murals, posters, and handicrafts, which were then displayed in public institutions. Writers produced a series of guidebooks about each state. Musicians, actors, and stage personnel formed WPA symphony orchestras, bands, and theater troupes that gave performances around the country.[45]

Other service projects came under the heading of "welfare activities." Housekeeping aide projects provided work for blue-collar women and assistance through home visits to relief families in times of illness or other emergencies. Public health projects were a source of work for skilled health professionals on relief (doctors, dentists, nurses, pharmacists), as well nonprofessional "helpers" in hospitals, clinics, and school s. And the pains taken to ensure a more than adequate supply of domestic service workers led to the development of a household-worker training project that provided training in domestic service. The service projects were an important source of work for women. Thus in the April 1938 survey, while women comprised 14 percent of the total WPA rolls, 41 percent were on white-collar projects—and 53 percent of all those on white-collar projects were women.[46]

The Continuing Saga of Production-for-Use

The results of the attack on production-for-use projects in the FERA were seen in the WPA. Production-for-use was still important, absorbing 11 percent of all WPA funds. And it continued to provide the main source of work for blue-collar women: in the April 1938 survey, 56 percent of the women on the WPA were working on production-for-use projects, where they made up a full 87 percent of all those on the projects.[47] Yet two of the innovative FERA projects—federal aid to cooperatives and putting idle workers to work in idle factories—remained buried. And the mattress-making project was not brought back until 1939, and then in a manner that seemed designed not to attract attention.

Sewing rooms remained by far the most important type of production-for-use project. Almost 383 million garments and 118 million household articles (e.g., towels and sheets), as well as hospital and institutional gowns, were produced. The sewing rooms became increasingly mechanized: cutting rooms were often centralized and foot treadle and electric machines replaced some of the hand sewing.[48]

The FERA's gardening and canning projects were also expanded in the WPA. As in the earlier programs, produce from community gardens was canned and preserved, and then distributed to relief families. The school lunch program was expanded as well. Using surplus agricultural commodities collected through the AAA's crop reduction program, along with food grown in relief gardens, over 1.2 billion lunches were served free or for a small fee to children from relief families.[49]

The WPA also continued FERA programs to distribute surplus commodities, primarily food, fuel, and goods produced in pro-

WPA production-for-use projects: women canning vegetables in Vermont; women teasing Spanish moss to fill mattresses in Savannah, Georgia; and a shoe repair project in a public school in New Jersey. [National Archives]

duction-for-use projects. Almost 95 million books were renovated, furniture was made for WPA nursery schools, shoes were
repaired, and books were copied into Braille.[50]

Despite the earlier fight against it, mattress-making was
brought back in 1939 and 1940: New Deal officials still considered
it important to find uses for some of the ever increasing surplus
cotton. Trying to avert the protest that had accompanied the
earlier project, mattress-making was now placed under the heading "Sewing and Mattress Projects," an apparent attempt to
portray it as just another labor-intensive sewing activity. Yet these
projects were as large as before, and 1.2 million mattresses were
produced in 1939.[51]

Some WPA production-for-use projects ran into trouble,
however. Proposals for slum clearance and demolition projects
were squelched by building wreckers, and complaints from com-
mercial exterminators led WPA administrators to abandon plans
for a rat extermination project. The continuing controversy even-
tually led to specific restrictions. The 1939 appropriation act
prohibited the WPA from using funds to establish "mills, factories, stores, or plants which would manufacture, handle, process,
or produce for sale articles, commodities, or products ... in
competition with existing industries," and the mattress projects
were later closed "in deference to the objections of private manufacturing interests."[52]

Nevertheless, production-for-use had its supporters, and as
the Depression wore on increasing numbers of people came to
question the wisdom of continually kowtowing to private enterprise. This sentiment was expressed by William H. Stead, acting
director of the United States Employment Service, in a 1939
address to the National Conference of Social Work:

> Perhaps we should begin to think of government work as an
> essential supplement to private enterprise in rounding out the
> production of goods and services needed for the "fuller life." It
> may be that we have reached the point where the main question
> is not whether public work competes with private enterprise, but

whether it adds to total over-all needed production—private and public combined.[53]

This approach—that government work should be a permanent supplement to private enterprise—never had a chance to be tested: war was coming, and the United States turned its attention to war production and the WPA to military projects. Increasing numbers of the construction projects involved work on airports. While more than 480 airports were built and another 470 improved throughout the WPA's eight years, almost 40 percent of this work was completed in the 1940s. Other projects included construction or repair of military establishments and "strategic" highways, as well as salvage operations in automobile "graveyards." Service and welfare projects were also adapted to war-related activities: education and recreation activities were developed for military personnel, while military clothing and other articles (tents, blankets, and knapsacks) were reconditioned.[54]

As war production expanded and unemployment fell, there was also an increased emphasis in vocational training programs, primarily in military industries. While women were as much the target of these projects as men, African-Americans continued to be slighted.[55]

REFORM AND REACTION IN 1939

Over the years opposition to the New Deal became more coherent, and the elections of November 1938 sent a large number of conservatives to Congress. When these newly elected senators and representatives took office in the spring of 1939, they immediately began to change or dismantle New Deal programs. One of the most important targets was the WPA.

While the changes made in the EWRP during the fall of 1934 in response to attacks from the business community were fundamentally economic, dealing with problems of interference with low-wage labor markets and the logic of production-for-profit, this time the attack was on both economic and political

Workers leaving a shipbuilding plant in Mobile, Alabama, that was mobilized for the war effort. (National Archives).

grounds. The nature of the changes was captured in the WPA's new name: instead of Works Progress Administration, it became Work Projects Administration, and would now be housed in the new Federal Works Agency. The changes that were economic in nature, discussed earlier in this chapter, were intended to further increase the supply of labor available to the private sector. They included the "18-month rule," no longer using prevailing wage rates to determine hours of work, and requiring WPA workers to accept private sector jobs even if the pay was lower than the amount they earned on the WPA. And the prohibition of projects in factories, mills, etc., was designed to reduce contradictions with the logic of production-for-profit.

The other changes were political. The preferences given to

veterans were expanded by extending them to unmarried widows of veterans and to wives of "unemployable" veterans.[56] In contrast, noncitizens and Communists were prohibited from participating in the program at all—they were considered "subversive" and a threat to national security. Although this prohibition was extended the following year to members of Nazi Bund organizations, it was primarily used against progressives, and, in fact, was the beginning of the attack that developed into the anti-Communist witchhunts after the war. Subversiveness was defined very broadly to include anyone who had signed a petition to place a nominee on a Communist Party ticket, had once belonged to a Communist organization, or, ominously, was "thought by responsible WPA officials to have done something that branded him [sic] as a Communist, a member of a Nazi Bund organization, or as otherwise 'subversive.'"[57] This was done despite the fact that none of these activities were illegal and the Communist Party was a recognized player on the political spectrum throughout the 1930s. WPA workers who failed to sign affidavits stating that they were not Communists or members of a Nazi organization were removed from the rolls, and even some who signed were accused of subversive activity and dismissed from the program. In New York City, widely considered a hotbed of leftist activity, 365 WPA workers were accused of being "subversive" and taken off the program, although most were later reinstated.[58]

This concern about Communists was the main reason for the termination of the Federal Theater Project. Even though the project was small in scale, the political nature of some of the productions aroused the ire of conservative congressmen. They were particularly troubled by a production called the *Living Newspaper*, which combined newsreel clips, radio shows, and acting to present contemporary issues from a progressive perspective. Conservatives were also upset by the fact that some of the productions were racially integrated. For instance, an investigator for the House Committee looking into WPA activities

Black and white actors in a play about prisoners in the south produced by the Federal Theater Project. [National Archives]

reported in May 1939 that in the play *Sing for Your Supper*, which was performed as part of the Federal Theater Project, "There is no distinction in the cast. The colored and white are mixed together, dance together, and the actors are the same."[59] Soon afterward Congress prohibited the use of federal funds for the entire Federal Arts Project. Sponsors were found in most states for the projects for writers, music, and art, but not for the theater projects, which ended with the termination of federal support.[60]

Thus the WPA continued. It was finally ended in June 1943 when mobilization for World War II substantially increased production and employment, and a shortage of labor for the time being ended the need for government programs in which people were put to work.

CONCLUSION: BRING BACK LARGE-SCALE VOLUNTARY WORK PROGRAMS

Nothing before or after the 1930s has matched the magnitude of the FERA, CWA, and WPA—programs that provided work each month for several million people, paid decent wages, and developed innovative projects in construction, the arts, and the production of consumer goods. Yet even though they were more restricted in scope, there were voluntary work programs before the Depression and such programs continued after it ended. In fact, job-creation programs have a long history in the United States. They were developed in many cities during recessions from the early 1800s through the early 1900s—primarily to provide work for white men. And as the 1930s programs wound down, a permanent voluntary program was recommended by the

National Resources Planning Board, a high-level federal commission appointed by President Roosevelt to develop overall economic plans for the post-World War II period. The board's final report called for an "economic bill of rights" that would ensure the basic necessities of life, including the right to a job provided by the government if the private sector failed to do so, and advocated the "formal *acceptance by the Federal Government of responsibility* for insuring jobs a decent pay to all those able to work regardless of whether or not they can pass a means test." This return to a program similar to the CWA would have been accomplished through a permanent "Work Administration" that would provide "*socially useful work* other than construction ... for the otherwise unemployed."[1]

The idea of a voluntary work program was kept alive through the 1940s and 1950s by organizations such as the National Manpower Council and the Upjohn Institute, which published books and reports discussing job creation, training, and education. The programs returned in the 1960s, when concern about long-term unemployment caused by changing job-skill requirements led to the 1962 Manpower Development and Training Administration (MDTA). The MDTA provided training and a stipend for unemployed workers; it initially targeted white male heads of household, but its focus shifted to African-American youths as the War On Poverty got underway in the middle of the decade. The MDTA was then surpassed by the Neighborhood Youth Corps and other War On Poverty programs, which provided work, education, training, and support services to pull people considered to be on the margins of society into the mainstream.

Voluntary work programs similar to those of the Depression were expanded in the 1970s. The recession of 1969-1970, which ended the long economic expansion of the 1960s, led to the Public Employment Program (PEP) in 1971. Three years later, the Comprehensive Employment and Training Act (CETA) replaced the PEP, the MDTA, and the War On Poverty work and training programs with one all-inclusive program. It included Public

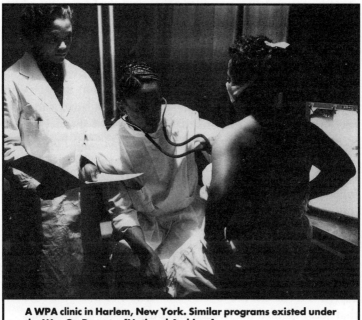

A WPA clinic in Harlem, New York. Similar programs existed under the War On Poverty. [National Archives]

Service Employment (PSE), which continued the job-creation program of the PEP.

While PEP and PSE marked the return of job creation, they were far more constrained than their 1930s' predecessors. Most important, they were only allowed to develop work in the service sector; the construction and production-for-use projects that were such critical components of the earlier programs were absent. Further, PEP and PSE were small in comparison to the earlier programs: at their high point in March 1978, only 742,000 people were involved. This was only one-sixth of the maximum reached during the 1930s—even though the labor force had doubled in the intervening years. And while the 1930s' programs, at their peak, created work for one-third of the unemployed, at its high point PSE provided jobs for only 12 percent of the jobless.

In spite of these constraints, the 1970s' programs were plagued by many of the same criticisms that surrounded the FERA, CWA, and WPA. Charges of inefficiency and make-work were the most frequent. They were accompanied by complaints that wages were too high and that the programs were too expensive. And, as in the 1930s, contradictory mandates meant that these criticisms were often accurate. When Ronald Reagan became President in 1981, he quickly eliminated PSE and allowed CETA to expire the following year. It was replaced by the much narrower Job Training Partnership Act (JTPA), which has provided short-term training to meet the needs of local employers.

It was therefore not until the 1980s that large-scale voluntary programs, especially those designed to create jobs, disappeared from the policy agenda and debates. The fact that the evaluation of these programs as unsound and unrealistic is generally accepted is a real tribute to the constriction of policy discussions that accompanied the Reagan and Bush right-wing agendas.

In place of voluntary work programs, the 1980s and 1990s have seen the proliferation of mandatory programs for welfare recipients. Training has usually been aimed at immediate job placement—primarily in low-wage service sector jobs that give people little chance to move out of poverty. And the core of these programs has been workfare, which requires recipients to "work off" their welfare payments. These highly stigmatized programs have been accompanied by cuts in (inflation-adjusted) payments, a variety of programs designed to alter the behavior of welfare recipients,[2] and prosecutions for "welfare fraud," in which recipients are charged with misdemeanors and felonies if they receive overpayments in their welfare checks. This has been done even though the overpayments are often due to mistakes made by the welfare department—which has been true, for instance, in approximately one-half of the cases in California.[3]

It is again time for a change. The "jobless recovery" from the deep recessions of the early 1990s has left millions of people unemployed and underemployed—and the severe cuts in government services have left a multitude of needs unmet. Instead of the mandatory and punitive work programs that characterized the 1980s and 1990s, we need to revive the entire range of voluntary work programs. Modeled on the innovated and extensive programs of the 1930s, these could create jobs in a variety of areas—for example, construction projects in light rail systems and low-cost housing, service work in recreation and education, and support for the arts. And lessons could be incorporated from the employment and training programs of the 1960s and 1970s, as well as from policies in effect in most other developed countries, so that the new programs would meet the needs of women and people of color, instead of focussing primarily on white men.

In order to give both women and men real choices about combining work in the home with jobs outside the home, we also need to develop progressive family and labor market policies. A comprehensive family policy would recognize the value of work in the home, and would include a family allowance that is not means-tested, national health care, federally subsidized child care, family and medical leave, flexible work hours, and an adequate supply of low-cost housing. (A minimal family leave policy was finally adopted in 1992 and a national health care program is imminent, both of which may provide the foundation for potentially more comprehensive policies in the future.) A higher minimum wage, pay equity, and anti-discrimination policies would help close the wage gaps between women and men and between people of color and whites. And free training and education through college would open jobs to people who have traditionally been underrepresented in them.

Money for these programs could come from a truly progressive income tax, a tax on the sale of assets held for a short period of time (which would also discourage speculation), and the military budget. And those responsible for the financial industry fiascos,

An WPA instructor teaching softball in South Carolina. Similar programs existed under CETA. [National Archives]

not the taxpayers, should be forced to repay the billions of dollars that they squandered.

At the center of these policies would be a voluntary government work program. In order to ensure that currently employed workers are not displaced and that unions are not undermined, the pay would be equal to that of other workers doing the same type of work and they would be allowed to join a union.

If such a program were instituted, it would probably again face a barrage of criticism, including the old ones of inefficiency and make-work. There are at least five types of responses that can be given to this attack.

First, many government services are seen an inefficient and/or as make-work simply because they are carried out by the government and not by private enterprise. Yet increasing efficiency often involves speed-ups and replacing workers with machines—something that has been happening with increasing frequency among white-collar as well as blue-collar workers. While this may cut costs and increase profits (in the short run), and thereby help owners, it is not beneficial for workers. Furthermore, the whole concept of make-work needs closer inspection. Are private sector jobs better than public sector jobs simply because they're based on production-for-profit? Are jobs that are created in sweatshops or fast food restaurants better than work in the public sector as a teacher's aide or than repairing bridges and roads?

Second, charges of inefficiency and make-work have followed from these programs' often contradictory mandates. This was particularly clear in the 1930s, when regulations that the projects use a maximum of labor and a minimum of machinery—in order to create jobs for as many of the unemployed as possible with the available funds—meant that the work was clearly inefficient by industry standards.

Third, job-creation programs do two important things: they provide jobs for people who are unemployed and underemployed, and they provide much-needed services. While this argument was made during the 1960s and 1970s, it disappeared during the 1980s. In fact, the dominance of right-wing economic policy—including the ballooning federal budget deficit—has led the general public to believe that we cannot afford many government services. However, we do have a choice. We can provide prenatal health care for poor women now—or spend much more later on intensive hospital care for sick infants. We can develop programs now for school drop-outs—or pay much more later for prisons. We can provide services befitting the richest country in the world—from libraries to roads and bridges to shelter the poor—or we can become a meaner society with increasingly endemic violence.

Fourth, these programs make good economic sense. The 1980s saw "trickle-down" economics, in which tax breaks were given to the rich, who were then supposed to increase investment and create jobs. However, most of this money was used for speculation in stocks and junk bonds, as well as for buying luxury goods. Instead, we need "bubble-up" economic policies, which direct money to people who will quickly spend it on goods and service. This will increase demand and lead business owners to increase production, hire more workers, and help get the economy going. (This "percolator" effect will not happen through President Bill Clinton's 1993 "economic stimulus" package, which was only a drop in the bucket. On the contrary: in conjunction with deficit reduction—which has mostly taken the form of further cuts in spending on services—it will bring about even more economic stagnation and unemployment.)

Fifth, and most fundamentally, the criteria that were used to evaluate past voluntary work programs must be challenged. Measure founded on the logic of production-for-profit need to be replaced by measures that are based on an assessment of people's needs. Since capitalist economic systems depend on unemployment to weaken labor—which keeps wages down and therefore increases profits—jobs are not normally created for everyone who wants to work. Thus voluntary programs that *make* work must be a basic component of our social welfare policies. History shows us that this is indeed possible.

NOTES

This book is based on extensive research on the New Deal work programs. Readers interested in more detailed citations should see my *Workfare or Fair Work: Women, Welfare, and Government Work Programs from the 1930s to the 1990s* (forthcoming from Rutgers University Press).

ABBREVIATIONS

Abbreviations of agencies

AAA	Agricultural Adjustment Act
CCC	Civilian Conservation Corps
CETA	Comprehensive Employment and Training Act
CWA	Civil Works Administration
EWRP	Emergency Work Relief Program
FERA	Federal Emergency Relief Administration
FSRC	Federal Surpus Relief Corporation
FWA	Federal Works Agency
NIRA	National Industrial Recovery Act
NRA	National Recovery Administration

PEP	Public Employment Program
PSE	Public Service Employment
PWA	Public Works Administration
WPA	Works Progress Administration

Abbreviations of reference sources

GPO	U.S. Government Printing Office, Washington, DC
NYT	*New York Times*
NA, RG 69	National Archives, Record Group 69: Records of the Works Projects Administration
FERA MR	*Monthly Report of the Federal Emergency Relief Administration*

CHAPTER 1: THE GREAT DEPRESSION

1. Richard B. Duboff, *Accumulation and Power: An Economic History of the United States* (Armonk, NY: M.E. Sharpe, 1989), pp. 87-88.
2. U.S. Bureau of the Census, *Historical Statistics of the United States, Colonial Times to 1970* (GPO, 1975), p. 126.
3. Lester V. Chandler, *America's Greatest Depression, 1929-1941* (New York: Harper and Row, 1970), pp. 4, 7, 21, 23.
4. William E. Leuchtenburg, *Franklin D. Roosevelt and the New Deal, 1932-1940* (New York: Harper Colyphon, 1963), p. 26.
5. An account of these activities can be found in Irving Bernstein, *The Lean Years: A History of the American Worker, 1920-1933* (Baltimore: Penguin Books, 1960); Louis Adamic, *My America, 1928-1938* (London: Hamish Hamilton, 1939); and David A. Shannon, *The Great Depression* (Englewood Cliffs, NJ: Prentice-Hall, 1960).
6. See Bernstein, *The Lean Years,* pp. 416-19; and Clark Kerr and Paul S. Taylor, "The Self-Help Cooperatives in California," in *Essays in Social Economics in Honor of Jessica Blanche Peixotto* (1935; Freeport, NY: Books for Libraries Press, Inc., 1967).
7. See John L. Shover, *Cornbelt Rebellion: The Farmers' Holiday Association* (Urbana: The University of Illinois Press, 1965).
8. For discussions of the unemployed councils, see Jeremy Brecher, *Strike!* (Boston: South End Press, 1977), ch. 5; Roy Rosensweig, "Radicals and the Jobless: The Musteites and the Unemployed Leagues, 1932-1936," *Labor History* 16 (Winter 1975): 52-77; and Frances Fox Piven and Richard A. Cloward, *Poor People's Movements: Why They Succeed, How They Fail* (New York: Vintage, 1979), ch. 2.
9. Adamic, *My America*, p. 309; Shannon, *The Great Depression*, pp. 119-20; and Bernstein, *The Lean Years*, pp. 422-23.

10. Bernstein, *The Lean Years*, pp. 432-34, ch. 13; and Arthur M. Schlesinger, Jr., *The Age of Roosevelt*. Vol. I: *The Crisis of the Old Order, 1919-1933* (Boston: Houghton Mifflin, 1957), pp. 256-65.

11. Dixon Wecter, *The Age of the Great Depression, 1929-1941* (New York: Macmillan, 1948), p. 36.

12. Quoted in Frances Fox Piven and Richard A. Cloward, *Regulating the Poor: The Functions of Public Welfare* (New York: Pantheon Books, 1971), p. 68.

13. Ibid., p. 60; Josephine Chapin Brown, *Public Relief, 1929-1939* (1940; New York: Octagon Books, 1971), pp. 138-39; and Schlesinger, *The Crisis of the Old Order*, p. 249.

14. Piven and Cloward, *Regulating the Poor*, p. 67.

15. Ibid, p. 56; and Edward A. Williams, *Federal Aid for Relief* (New York: Columbia University Press, 1939), pp. 19-20.

16. U.S., Congress, House, *Hearings before the House Committee on Labor, HR 206, 6011, 8088, HJ Res 164*, 72nd Cong., 2d sess., 1 February 1932.

17. Piven and Cloward, *Regulating the Poor*, pp. 51-52; Brown, *Public Relief*, pp. 68-71, 124-28; Williams, *Federal Aid for Relief*, pp. 24-35, 43-45; and Schlesinger, *The Crisis of the Old Order*, pp. 236-38.

18. Discussions of the first one hundred days can be found in Schlesinger, *The Age of Roosevelt*. Vol. 2: *The Coming of the New Deal*, chs. 1-10, 17, and 19; and Leuchtenburg, *Franklin D. Roosevelt and the New Deal*, chs. 3 and 4.

19. Alfred Edgar Smith, *Negro Project Workers: An Annual Report of Matters I I Incident to the Administration of Race Relations in Federal Unemployment Relief for the Year 1936* (January 1937), in NA, RG 69, WPA Series 11, #102: Public Relations. In February 1935 a decimal classification system was adopted for FERA, CWA, and WPA records in the National Archives. Documents obtained before this time were included in the CWA Series #2 (hereafter CWA Series 2) and the FERA Old General Subject Series #8 (FERA Series 8), while documents gathered after this date were filed in FERA New General Subject Series #9 (FERA Series 9) and series for each state (FERA Series 10). The decimal classification system was continued in the WPA in the General Subject Series #11 (WPA Series 11) and in the State Series #12 (WPA Series 12).

20. Accounts of the situation of blacks during the Depression can be found in Raymond Wolters, *The Negro and the Depression: The Problem of Economic Recovery* (Westport, CT: Greenwood Publishing, 1970) and Jacqueline Jones, *Labor of Love, Labor of Sorrow: Black Women, Work, and the Family from Slavery to the Present* (New York: Basic Books, 1985), ch. 6.

21. Schlesinger, *The Coming of the New Deal*, p. 5.

CHAPTER 2: FEDERAL UNEMPLOYMENT RELIEF

1. Schlesinger, *The Coming of the New Deal,* p. 275.
2. *FERA MR,* 22 May–30 June 1933, p. 19.
3. "Rules and Regulations No. 2," in ibid., pp. 11-12.
4. Ibid, p. 12.
5. Brown, *Public Relief,* p. 233.
6. Arthur E. Burns, "Federal Emergency Relief Administration," in *The Municipal Yearbook 1937: The Authoritative Resume of Activities and Statistical Data of American Cities,* eds. Clarence E. Ridley and Orin F. Nolting (Chicago: The International City Managers' Association, 1937), p. 397.
7. In 1935 the College Student Aid Program was replaced by the National Youth Administration and the exemption continued to hold.
8. Alfred E. Smith, "The Negro and Relief," *FERA MR* (March 1936): 10-17.
9. These practices are described in several of Alfred Edgar Smith's "Reports of Activities" and "Highlights of Activities" in NA, RG 69, WPA Series 11, #102: Public Relations.
10. "Administration Series - 28," in Doris Carothers, WPA Research Monograph VI, *Chronology of the Federal Emergency Relief Administration, May 12, 1933, to December 31, 1935* (GPO, 1937; New York: Da Capo Press, 1971), p. 24.
11. "Relief for White-Collar Workers," *FERA MR* (December 1935): 60.
12. "Rules and Regulations No. 3," in Carothers, *Chronology of the FERA,* p. 9.
13. "Rules and Regulations No. 4," in ibid., p. 12.
14. Arthur E. Burns, "Work Relief Wage Policies, 1930-1936," *FERA MR* (June 1936): 33.
15. Smith, "The Negro and Relief," p. 14; NA, RG 69, CWA Series 2: Interracial Correspondence; and Donald S. Howard, *The WPA and Federal Relief Policy* (1943; New York: DaCapo Press, 1973), p. 292.
16. Cited in Mary Elizabeth Pidgeon, *Bulletin of the Women's Bureau,* No. 130, "Employed Women Under N.R.A. Codes" (GPO, 1935; New York: DaCapo Press, 1975), p. 13.
17. North Carolina Emergency Relief Commission, *Emergency Relief in North Carolina: A Record of the Development and the Activities of the North Carolina Emergency Relief Administration, 1932-1935* (Edwards and Broughton Company, 1936), p. 51.
18. This survey, which explored many aspects of relief, was done in May 1934. See "The Supplementing of Private Earnings by Relief," *FERA MR* (June 1935): 9; and also Burns, "The FERA," p. 397; and Brown, *Public Relief,* pp. 266-68.
19. FERA, *Proceedings of the Conference on Emergency Needs of Women* (GPO, 20 November 1933), pp. 11, 13, 27.

20. "Rules and Regulations No. 3" and "Rules and Regulations No. 8," in Carothers, *Chronology of the FERA*, pp. 9-10, 25; WPA, *Final Statistical Report of the Federal Emergency Relief Administration* (GPO, 1942), pp. 70-74; "Transient Program," *FERA MR* (December 1933): 11-12; and Ellery F. Reed, *Federal Transient Program: An Evaluative Survey May to July, 1934* (New York. NY: The Committee on Care of Transient and Homeless, 1934).

21. "Rules and Regulations No. 8," in Carothers, *Chronology of the FERA*, p. 25.

22. FERA, Division of Self-Help Cooperatives, *Self-Help Cooperatives: An Introductory Study* (GPO, 1934); and Kerr and Taylor, "The Self-Help Cooperatives in California."

23. "Emergency Education Program," *FERA MR* (June 1935): 16-19; "Rural School Continuation Program," *FERA MR* (October 1935): 21-24; WPA, *Final Statistical Report of the FERA*, pp. 59-63; and NA, RG 69, Series 8: Worker Education, FERA 1933.

24. FERA, *Proceedings of the Conference on the Emergency Needs of Women* (The White House, 20 November 1933), pp. 11-14.

25. "Women's Work Program," *FERA MR* (December 1933): 8.

26. The Drought Relief Program was subsumed under the Resettlement Administration in June 1935. See "Special Aid for Drought Sections," *FERA MR* (December 1933): 8; and Carothers, *Chronology of the FERA*, p. 19.

27. Janet Poppendieck, *Breadlines Knee-Deep in Wheat: Food Assistance in the Great Depression* (New Brunswick, NJ: Rutgers University Press, 1986), ch. 7; "Report of the Federal Surplus Relief Corporation," *FERA MR* (December 1933): 39-45; and "The Federal Surplus Relief Corporation," *FERA MR* (July 1935): 17-30.

CHAPTER 3: THE CIVIL WORKS ADMINISTRATION

1. This was seen in the *Business Week* index of economic activity, which increased approximately 40 percent from March through June 1933, and then fell 15 percent from June through September. See *Business Week*, 7 October 1934, p. 2.

2. Chandler, *America's Greatest Depression, 1929-1941*, pp. 48-49.

3. FERA press release in Carothers, *Chronology of the FERA*, p. 33.

4. See Arthur W. Macmahon, John D. Millett, and Gladys Ogden, *The Administration of Federal Work Relief* (New York: Da Capo Press, 1971), p. 35, for in-depth discussions of these issues.

5. "Chicago to Employ Lottery for Jobs," *NYT*, 2 December 1933, p. 30; and C. M. Bookman, "FERA Yesterday-Today-Tomorrow," *The Survey* (June 1934): 196.

6. "Civil Works Plan Stirs New England," *NYT*, 26 November 1933, Part IV, p. 1; "New York City CWA Swamped with Applicants," *NYT*, 28 November

1933, p. 26; "2000 for 299 Jobs Rioted at Dayton," *NYT*, 24 December 1933, Part IV, p. 1; and Schlesinger, *The Coming of the New Deal*, p. 273.

7. FERA, *Proceedings of the Conference on Emergency Needs of Women.*

8. Telegram from Hopkins, in Carothers, *Chronology of the FERA*, p. 34, and "Women's Work Series - 6," in ibid., p.35.

9. "Women's Division," *FERA MR* (July 1935): 44.

10. "FWCA Rules and Regulations No. 1," in Carothers, *Chronology of the FERA*, p. 28.

11. Compounding this problem, since the program was ended so soon many of the CWA projects were never finished or were completed only after a long delay, evoking criticism for waste and lack of planning. See Corrington Gill, "The Civil Works Administration," in *The Municipal Yearbook 1937*, pp. 426, 431; and U.S., Congress, House, *Hearings before the Subcommittee of the House Committee on Appropriations in Charge of Deficiency Appropriations*, H.R. 7527, 73rd Cong., 2d sess., 30 January 1934, p. 28. More recently, Bonnie Fox Schwartz has claimed that the involvement of engineers in planning CWA projects meant that they were more efficient and less like make-work compared to the early FERA. See Bonnie Fox Schwartz, *The CWA, 1933-1934: The Business of Emergency Employment in the New Deal* (Princeton: Princeton University Press, 1984).

12. Gill, "The Civil Works Administration," pp. 424-31.

13. Ibid.

14. Ibid.

15. "Education Series - 15," in Carothers, *Chronology of the FERA*, p. 42.

16. "FCWA Rules and Regulations No. 6," in Carothers, *Chronology of the FERA*, p. 33; and Arthur E. Burns, "Work Relief Wage Policies," pp. 33, 37-38.

17. U.S., Congress, House, *Hearings before the Committee on Expenditures in Executive Departments*, H.R. 7527, 73rd Cong., 2d sess., 13 February 1934, p. 16.

18. "FCWA Rules and Regulations No. 1," in Carothers, *Chronology of the FERA*, pp. 28-30; and "Women's Work Division - 6," in ibid., p. 35.

19. NA, RG 69, CWA Series 2: Interracial Correspondence.

20. Ibid.

21. Williams, *Federal Aid for Relief*, p. 122.

22. NA, RG 69, CWA Series 2: Commendations on CWA Program.

23. Interview with Arthur Goldschmidt, head of Professional Service Projects in the FERA and assistant to Jacob Baker in the CWA, New York City, 15 October 1981.

24. Since the 1933 average hourly wage for production workers in manufacturing was $.44, it is likely that in some areas CWA wage rates were higher than industrial private sector rates. See U.S. Bureau of the Census, *Historical Statistics of the United States, Colonial Times to 1970*, Series D 802-810,

"Earnings and Hours of Production Workers in Manufacturing: 1909 to 1970," p. 170.

25. For example, U.S., Congress, House, *Hearings before the Subcommittee of the House Committee on Appropriations in Charge of Deficiency Appropriations, H.R. 7527,* 73rd Cong., 2d sess., 30 January 1934, pp. 37-38; U.S., Congress, House, *Hearings before the Committee on Expenditures in Executive Departments, H.R. 7527,* 73rd Cong., 2d sess., 13 February 1934, pp. 14-15; *Time,* 1 January 1934, p. 10; and Gill, "The CWA," p. 431.

26. *The Nation,* 27 December 1933, p. 727; and "More Jobs Wanted," *The Nation,* 3 January 1934, p. 7.

27. This statement was excerpted from a proposal submitted to the Democratic and Republican State Committees for inclusion in their 1934 platforms. See Stephen Raushenbush, "Common Sense Follows the CWA," *The Nation,* 18 April 1934, p. 444.

28. The initial policy was amended five days later to allow people in predominantly urban counties to also work twenty-four hours per week. See telegram from Hopkins, in Carothers, *Chronology of the FERA,* p. 41.

29. Burns, "Work Relief Wage Policies," p. 37.

30. *Time,* 5 February 1934, p. 17; "Not Back to Hoover, Please!" *The Nation,* 28 March 1934, p. 346; "Lehman Appeals for More CWA Aid," *NYT,* 23 January 1934, p. 2; and "Roosevelt Studies Longer CWA Term," *NYT,* 3 February 1934, p. 1.

CHAPTER 4: THE NEW FERA

1. Hours of work were initially limited to twenty-four per week but raised to thirty two months later. See "Rural Rehabilitation Program-1," and Telegram, Mimeo, 2347, in Carothers, *Chronology of the FERA,* pp. 51, 57; and "The Rural Rehabilitation Program," *FERA MR* (August 1935): 14-20.

2. *Brown, Public Relief,* p. 235.

3. "Work Division - 9," in Carothers, *Chronology of the FERA,* p. 61.

4. "Work Division - 16," in ibid., p. 63.

5. "Relief for White-Collar Workers," *FERA MR* (December 1935): 60.

6. "Women's Division," *FERA MR* (July 1935): 44.

7. "Administrative Series - 71," in Carothers, *Chronology of the FERA,* p. 69.

8. Katherine D. Wood, WPA Research Monograph IV, *Urban Workers on Relief: Part II - The Occupational Characteristics of Workers on Relief in 79 Cities, May 1934* (GPO, 1936), p. 72.

9. The percentage of transient families increased during this time from approximately 15 percent of the cases to slightly more than 20 percent. See "Transient Relief," in WPA, *Final Statistical Report of the FERA,* pp. 70-74.

10. "Work Division Series - 1," Telegram, Mimeo, 1734, in Carothers, *Chronology of the FERA*, pp. 49, 52; and Brown, *Public Relief*, pp. 241-42.

11. "Work Division Series - 1," in Carothers, *Chronology of the FERA*, p. 49; and Burns, "Work Relief Wage Policies," p. 40.

12. Thus average monthly payments rose from approximately $14 a month under early FERA to $27 a month under the EWRP. See Burns, "Work Relief Wage Policies," pp. 33 and 43.

13. "Emergency Work Program," *FERA MR* (March 1934): 5; and Arthur E. Burns, "Federal Emergency Relief Administration," in *The Municipal Yearbook 1937*, p. 396.

14. This term was suggested by Eric Nilsson.

15. WPA, *Final Statistical Report of the FERA*, pp. 56-57.

16. "Relief for White-Collar Workers," *FERA MR* (December 1935): 59-64; and "List of Working Procedures for FERA Work Projects," in Carothers, *Chronology of the FERA*, p. 111.

17. "List of Working Procedures," Carothers, *Chronology of the FERA*, pp. 110-11.

18. "Work Division Series - 3," in Carothers, *Chronology of the FERA*, pp. 50-51; and P.A. Kerr, "Production-for-Use and Distribution in Work Relief Activities," *FERA MR* (September 1935): 5.

19. Kerr, "Production-for-Use," p. 5.

20. "Rural Rehabilitation - 1," in Carothers, *Chronology of the FERA*, p. 51; and Kerr, "Production-for-Use," pp. 3, 5.

21. The 12 million figure was for cattle processed as of January 1, 1935. See Kerr, "Production-for-Use," pp. 7-9.

22. U.S., Congress, Senate, *Hearings before the Committee on Agriculture and Forestry, on S. 2500, A bill to aid in relieving the existing national emergency through the free distribution to the needy of cotton and cotton products,* 73rd Cong., 2d sess., 9 February 1934; and Leuchtenburg, *Franklin D. Roosevelt and the New Deal*, pp. 72-73.

23. "Women's Division No. 41," in Carothers, *Chronology of the FERA*, p. 60; Kerr, "Production-for-Use," pp. 10-11; and press releases, NA, RG 69, FERA Series 9, #371: Production of Goods.

24. Kerr, "Production-for-Use," pp. 7-9; and "Instructions for Production of Sheepskin Coats," NA, RG 69, FERA Series 9, #371: Production of Goods.

25. Kerr, "Production-for-Use," p. 12; Joanna C. Colcord, "Ohio Produces for Ohioans," *The Survey* 70, no. 12 (December 1934): 371-73; Raymond G. Swing, "EPIC and the Ohio Plan," *The Nation*, 3 October 1934, pp. 379-81; and "Operation of Idle Factories," *Monthly Labor Review* (December 1934): 1311-19.

26. Robert E. Sherwood, *Roosevelt and Hopkins*, Vol. I (New York: Bantam Books, 1948), p. 70. There may well have been other leased factories, but it

is difficult to tell from the FERA reports whether a project was a leased factory or a labor-intensive workroom.

27. Kerr, "Production-for-Use," pp. 2-12.

28. "Factories for Idle Win Capitol Favor," *NYT*, 14 June 1934, p. 19; "Processing Plants to be Used in Relief," *NYT*, 22 June 1934, p. 2; "Canning Included in Federal Relief," *NYT*, 16 July 1934, p. 4.; "North Carolina Plans to Raise Rabbits and Guinea Pigs, Mine Coal and Can Beef," *NYT*, 26 August 1934, Sect. IV, p. 6; "Shops in Washington Planned for Needy," *NYT*, 15 July 1934, p. 3; "FERA Factories," *Business Week*, 28 July 1934, p. 22; and "Work Division Series - 13," in Carothers, *Chronology of the FERA*, p. 62.

CHAPTER 5: THE ATTACK ON WORK RELIEF

1. Arthur M. Schlesinger, Jr., The Age of Roosevelt. Vol. III: *The Politics of Upheaval* (Boston: Houghton Mifflin, 1960), ch. 4; and Leuchtenburg, *Franklin D. Roosevelt and the New Deal*, pp. 96-99 and 179-80.

2. Sinclair did not do too badly, receiving 880,000 votes compared to 1,139,000 for the winner, Merriam, and 303,000 for a third candidate. See Schlesinger, *The Politics of Upheaval*, ch. 7; Leuchtenburg, *Franklin D. Roosevelt and the New Deal*, pp. 114-15; "Upton Sinclair's Utopia," *The Nation*, 21 February 1934, pp. 226-27; and Raymond G. Swing, "Last Look at the Election," *The Nation*, 7 November 1934, pp. 529-30.

3. Schlesinger, *The Politics of Upheaval*, ch. 3; and Leuchtenburg, *Franklin D. Roosevelt and the New Deal*, pp. 103-6.

4. Approximately 1.17 million workers went on strike in 1933, and about 1.47 million did so the following year. See Bureau of the Census, *Historical Statistics of the United States, Colonial Times to 1970*, Series D 970-985, "Work Stoppages, Workers Involved, Man-Days Idle, Major Issues, and Average Duration: 1881 to 1970," p. 179.

5. There are a number of exciting accounts of these strikes. See, for example, Bernstein, *The Turbulent Years: A History of the American Worker, 1933-1941* (Boston: Houghton Mifflin, 1971), chs. 2-6; Richard O. Boyer and Herbert M. Morais, *Labor's Untold Story* (New York: United Electrical, Radio & Machine Workers of America, 1955), ch. 9; and Jeremy Brecher, *Strike!*, ch. 5.

6. The automobile and steel strikes were led by the CIO (Committee for Industrial Organizations). Formed in 1935 to organize throughout industries—instead of along craft union lines, as was done in the American Federation of Labor (AFL)— the CIO formally split from the AFL three years later.

7. "2,700 in Strike Row on Civil Works Job," *NYT*, 5 December 1933, p. 2; James Rorty, "America on the Work Dole," *The Nation*, 27 June 1934, pp.

723-26; "Relief Workers Fight," *Social Work Today* 1, no. 3 (July-August 1934): 17; "600 Rioters Here Battle 100 Police at Relief Bureau," *NYT*, 27 May 1934, p. 1; "50 Are Hurt in Riot of Los Angeles Idle," *NYT*, 2 June 1934, p. 5; "Gun Battle Kills Two in Ohio Relief Riot," *NYT*, 14 July 1934, p. 1; "30 Relief Rioters Injured in Phoenix," *NYT*, 7 September 1934, p. 3; and "'Hunger Marchers' Routed at Albany; Rioting in Denver," *NYT*, 31 October 1934, pp. 1, 14.

8. Jones, *Labor of Love, Labor of Sorrow*, pp. 203-4; Bernstein, *The Turbulent Years*, p. 151; and Leuchtenburg, *Franklin D. Roosevelt and the New Deal*, p. 138.

9. Schlesinger, *The Politics of Upheaval*, ch. 2; and Leuchtenburg, *Franklin D. Roosevelt and the New Deal*, pp. 100-3.

10. Schlesinger, *The Coming of the New Deal*, pp. 486-87.

11. The persistent complaints that workers were choosing relief instead of private-sector jobs led to a 1935 survey which found that only 3 percent of "alleged job refusals" could be attributed to "unjustified" causes that might have been related to work relief. See "Alleged Refusal by Relief Clients to Accept Employment," *FERA MR* (June 1935): 1-8; and "Summary Study of Alleged Job Refusals by Relief Persons," *FERA MR* (November 1935): 6-10.

12. *Congressional Digest* (January 1935): 27-28.

13. Nels Anderson, *The Right to Work* (New York: Modern Age Books, 1938), p. 65.

14. Letter from J.C. Lindsey to Perry A. Fellows, Administrative Office, FERA, 10 December 1934, in NA, FERA Series 8: Goods, Production of, for Unemployed.

15. *Congressional Digest* (January 1935): 29.

16. "FERA Factories," *Business Week*, 28 July 1934, p. 22.

17. Anderson, *The Right to Work*, p. 92.

18. Ibid., p. 99.

19. Harry L. Hopkins, *Spending to Save: The Complete Story of Relief* (New York: W. W. Norton, 1936), p. 125.

20. This was reflected in the *Business Week* index of economic activity. After fluctuating between approximately 64 and 67 from late December 1933 through late June 1934, the index fell from 67 to 57 between late June and late August. See *Business Week*, 15 October 1934, p. 2; and Bureau of the Census, *Historical Statistics of the United States*, Series D 1-10, "Labor Force and Its Components: 1900 to 1947," p. 126.

21. "Hopkins Tightens Spending on Relief," *NYT*, 8 September 1934, p. 16; and "Administrative Orders - 18," in Carothers, *Chronology of the FERA*, p. 66.

22. "Administrative Series - 17," in Carothers, *Chronology of the FERA*, p. 22.

23. NA, RG 69, FERA Series 8: Strikers, Relief to; and "Strikers Denied Relief," *Social Work Today* 1, no. 3 (July-August 1934): 17.

24. James Myers, "Relief for Strikers Families," *The Survey* 70, no. 10 (October 1934): 307-8; "Shall the Government Feed Strikers?" *The Nation*, 12 September 1934, p. 285; "Maine Poor Overseers Bar Food to Strikers," *NYT*, 6 September 1934, p. 2; "Jersey Aid Board Bars General Strike Relief," *NYT*, 8 September 1934, p. 1; and Bernstein, *The Turbulent Years*, p. 312.

25. "Administrative Series - 17 Amendment," in Carothers, *Chronology of the FERA*, p. 65; "Rise in Strike Idle Seen," *NYT*, 19 September 1934, p. 3; "State Relief Planned," *NYT*, 20 September 1934, p. 3.

26. "Removal from Relief Rolls to Meet Labor Shortages," *FERA MR* (July 1935): 49.

27. Letter from Thad Holt to Harry Hopkins, 21 September 1934, in NA, RG 69, FERA Series 8: Cotton Reports.

28. "Removal from Relief Rolls to Meet Labor Shortages," *FERA MR* (July 1935): 49; "States and Cities Directed to Pay Full Relief Share," *NYT*, 22 September 1934, p. 1.

29. "Administrative Orders Series - 21," in Carothers, *Chronology of the FERA*, pp. 68-69.

30. Edward Ainsworth Williams, *Federal Aid for Relief*, p. 126; and "Minimum Pay Rate Ends on Relief Jobs; Local Scales Replace FERA's 30-Cent Rule," *NYT*, 23 November 1934, p. 2.

31. "Survey of Common Labor Rates Paid on the Work Program," *FERA MR* (January 1935): 5, 7; and Burns, "Work Relief Wage Policies," p. 41.

32. James Rorty, "The Relief Business Is Booming," *The Nation*, 22 August 1934, p. 206.

33. "Relief from Relief Industry," *Business Week*, 20 October 1934, p. 7.

34. Colcord, "Ohio Produces for Ohioans," p. 371.

35. "Administrative Series - 62" and "Work Division Series - 20," in Carothers, *Chronology of the FERA*, pp. 65-66; and Williams, *Federal Aid for Relief*, p. 146.

36. Harry A. Millis and Royal E. Montgomery, *The Economics of Labor*. Vol. II: *Labor's Risks and Social Insurance* (New York: McGraw-Hill, 1938), pp. 116-18; and State Relief Administration of California, *Review of Activities of the State Relief Administration of California, 1933-1935* (Sacramento, CA: California State Printing Office, 1936), p. 201.

37. Cited in Sherwood, *Roosevelt and Hopkins*, Vol. I, p. 70. While the FERA was deluged with complaints about alleged unfair competition from the mattress projects, some mattress manufacturers sent letters with offers to rent their idle factories to the FERA. NA, RG 69, FERA Series 8: Mattress Projects, Complaints re, and Mattress Projects, General Correspondence re Operation of.

38. Anderson, *The Right to Work*, p. 56.

39. FERA Press Release No. 922, in Carothers, *Chronology of the FERA*, p. 66.

40. "Retailers Attack Relief Activities," *NYT*, 9 September 1934, Sect. II, p. 8; "Factories for Idle Fought as Unsound," *NYT*, 8 October 1934, p. 11; "Production for Use," *The Survey* (October 1934): 328; "Relief Business," *Business Week*, 15 September 1934, p. 9; and "Relief from Relief Industry," *Business Week*, 20 October 1934, p. 7.

41. "Relief from Relief Industry"; "Retailers Attack Relief Activities"; "Factories for Idle Fought as Unsound"; and Anderson, *The Right to Work*, pp. 112-13.

42. For example, electricity rates declined by 34.1 percent for 240 kilowatt hours per month in Knoxville. See *The Nation*, 10 October 1934, p. 405.

43. Jacob Baker, "Work Relief: The Program Broadens," *NYT*, 11 November 1934, Sect. VI, p. 6.

44. "Opposes Housing as Competitive," *NYT*, 23 September 1934, Sect. XI, p. 2.

45. *Congressional Digest* (January 1935): 11-12.

CHAPTER 6: THE SOCIAL SECURITY ACT AND THE WPA

1. Frances Perkins, Secretary of Labor during the New Deal, stated that "...the opposition was so great from the American Medical Association (principally) that it would have killed the whole Social Security Act if [national health insurance] had been passed at that time." See Frances Perkins, "Introduction," in Edwin Witte, *The Development of the Social Security Act* (Madison, WI: University of Wisconsin Press, 1962), p. viii.

2. Maxwell S. Stewart, *Social Security* (New York: W. W. Norton, 1937), p. 190. Parallels exist between the FERA and the Social Security Act compared to the National Industrial Recovery Act (NIRA) and the National Labor Relations Act (also known as the Wagner Act). Both the FERA and the NIRA were passed during the first one hundred days of the New Deal. The FERA served as a model for the permanent Social Security Act, passed by the Senate in June 1935 during the second one hundred days and signed into law two months later; while the NIRA led to the permanent National Labor Relations Act, also passed in June 1935. In both the Social Security Act and the National Labor Relations Act, many of the problems (for capitalists) of the earlier acts had been eliminated.

3. Paul H. Douglas, *Social Security in the United States: An Analysis and Appraisal of the Federal Social Security Act* (New York: McGraw-Hill, 1936), pp. 100-101.

4. U.S., Congress, House, *Hearings before the Committee on Ways and Means, 21 January - 12 February 1935, on H.R. 4120, The Economic Security Act*, 74th Cong., 1st sess., p. 25.

5. "What About a Permanent Plan?" *The Survey* (December 1934): 391.

6. Ibid.; and "The Business of Federal Relief," *The Survey* (January 1935): 24.

7. "Permanent Relief Asked by Mayors from Roosevelt," *NYT*, 23 September 1934, p. 1; "The Mayors Confer with the President," *The American City* (October 1934): 39; and "Mayors Demand Vast New Works," *NYT*, 25 November 1934, p. 2.

8. "Hopkins Envisions New Era in Relief," *NYT*, 24 August 1934, p. 17.

9. Macmahon, Millett, and Ogden, *The Administration of Federal Work Relief*, p. 26.

10. "Flurry Over Hopkins Finds His ‹EPIA› at Work," *NYT*, 2 December 1934, Sect. IV, p. 1.

11. Macmahon, Millett, and Ogden, *The Administration of Federal Work Relief*, p. 27.

12. This is what Roosevelt meant when, in his speech introducing the Social Security Act to Congress, he declared that "the Federal Government must and shall quit this business of relief." See "H[ouse]. Doc. No. 1, 74th Cong., 1st sess.," in Carothers, *Chronology of the FERA*, p. 70.

13. "Survey of Cases Removed from Relief Rolls," *FERA MR* (January 1936): 26, 27, 37; Howard, *The WPA*, p. 57; Arthur E. Burns and Edward A. Williams, WPA Research Monograph XXIV, *Federal Work, Security, and Relief Programs* (GPO, 1941), p. 111; Lincoln Fairley, "Survey of Former Emergency Relief Administration Cases in New Jersey," *FERA MR* (June 1936): 100.

14. Brown, *Public Relief*, p. 380; Fairley, "Survey of Former Emergency Relief Administration Cases," pp. 107-8; and Edward A. Williams, "Legal Settlement in the United States," *FERA MR* (August 1935): 33-40; Howard, *The WPA*, pp. 73-77, 338; and Williams, *Federal Aid for Relief*, p. 149.

15. Corrington Gill, "Local Work for Relief," *Survey Midmonthly* (May 1940).

16. Fairley, "Survey of Former Emergency Relief Administration Cases," p. 107; and Howard, *The WPA*, p. 99.

17. In order to ensure that they had enough supervisors and workers with specific skills, 10 percent of those on a project could be hired through the labor market instead of taken from the relief rolls, although throughout an entire state only 5 percent could fit this category. See "Executive Order 7046," in Carothers, *Chronology of the FERA*, p. 80; and FWA, *Final Report on the WPA Program, 1935-1943* (GPO, 1947; rept. ed., Westport, CT: Greenwood Press, 1976), p. 16.

18. Some flexibility was always allowed in the determination of total monthly payments and hourly rates. Regions could be redefined, usually to a more urban classification, and rates for any occupational group could be raised or lowered up to 10 percent in order to bring them more closely in line with private industry. Most importantly, by 1939 the extremely low rates for unskilled workers in the southern region had been increased by approxi-

mately 50 percent. See Burns, "Work Relief Wage Policies," pp. 43-54; and FWA, *Final Report on the WPA*, pp. 23-25.

19. FWA, *Final Report on the WPA*, pp. 23-25; Macmahon, Millett, and Ogden, *The Administration of Federal Work Relief*, pp. 151-57; and Howard, *The WPA*, ch. 6.

20. FWA, *Final Report on the WPA*, pp. 23-25; Howard, *The WPA*, pp. 214-16; and Macmahon, Millett, and Ogden, *The Administration of Federal Work Relief*, pp. 157-61.

21. Howard, *The WPA*, pp. 215-16; and FWA, *Final Report on the WPA*, p. 27.

22. Howard, *The WPA*, p. 199.

23. Ibid., pp. 490-92; and FWA, *Final Report on the WPA*, pp. 23-25.

24. The eighteen-month rule was amended as the economy improved. For fiscal years 1942 and 1943, workers were dismissed from the rolls only if there were others with similar skills who had been waiting three or more months for a WPA placement. And those removed from the rolls could become eligible again after twenty days instead of the original thirty. See FWA, *Final Report on the WPA*, p. 21; and Howard, *The WPA*, pp. 519-22.

25. FWA, *Final Report on the WPA*, p. 41.

26. Ibid., p. 27.

27. Cited in Howard, *The WPA*, p. 278.

28. Ibid., p. 279.

29. FWA, *Final Report on the WPA*, p. 17. In addition, large families were generally given preference over those with few or no dependents. See Howard, *The WPA*, pp. 346-50.

30. Howard, *The WPA*, p. 279.

31. FWA, *Report on Progress of the WPA Program*, 30 June 1941, p. 51; and Howard, *The WPA*, pp. 279-80.

32. Commenting on this practice in its 1937 report, the National Association for the Advancement of Colored People argued that proportionately fewer blacks than whites should be taken off the rolls because they experienced such severe discrimination in private industry. Cited in Smith, "Highlights of Activities," July 1938, p. 14.

33. Ibid., and Howard, *The WPA*, p. 292.

34. Smith, *Negro Project Workers*, pp. 4-6; and Howard, *The WPA*, pp. 291-93.

35. Smith, "Highlights of Activities," September 1938, p. 3.

36. FWA, *Final Report on the WPA*, p. 45. In addition, .4 percent of those on the rolls were "other."

37. Smith, *Negro Project Workers*, p. 9.

38. Smith, *Negro Press Digest*, 16 January 1937, p. 1-A, in NA, RG 69, WPA Series 11, #102: Public Relations.

39. Smith, "Highlights of Activities," May 1937, p. 6.

40. Ibid.

41. Smith, "Highlights of Activities," August 1937, p. 8.

42. FWA, *Final Report of the WPA*, p. 122.

43. Ibid., pp. 131-32.

44. Smith, "Highlights of Activities," June 1936 through November 1936; and Jones, *Labor of Love, Labor of Sorrow*, p. 219.

45. FWA, *Final Report on the WPA*, pp. 60-67, 122.

46. Ibid., pp. 44, 68-70, 133; and NA, RG 69, WPA Series 11, #212.2: Welfare Projects, and #230: Women's Work.

47. FWA, *Final Report of the WPA*, pp. 44, 122.

48. Ibid., pp. 67, 122, 133; and *Trend of Developments in the Sewing and Mattress Program*, pp. 2-3, in NA, RG 69, WPA Series 11, #218.1: Sewing and Mattress Projects, 1940.

49. FWA, *Final Report on the WPA*, pp. 68, 122, 133; and Bureau of Agricultural Economics, *The School Lunch Program and Agricultural Surplus Disposal* (October 1941), in NA, RG 69, WPA Series 11, #212.2: School Lunch Program.

50. FWA, *Final Report on the WPA*, pp. 68-70, 133; and NA, RG 69, WPA Series 11, #212.2: Welfare Projects, WPA.

51. *Trend of Developments*, p. 2. Other uses were also found for some of the surplus cotton: for instance, in addition to the workrooms, farm families were given surplus cotton to make their own mattresses. A pamphlet, *Make—or Buy—a Mattress: Turn Surplus Cotton into Better Living*, was distributed by the Department of Agriculture, and a program, "From Bales to Beds," was broadcast on the radio. See NA, RG 69, WPA Series 11, #212.1: Mattress Manufacture, 1940.

52. Howard, *The WPA*, pp. 133-34; FWA, *Final Report on the WPA*, p. 68.

53. "The Federal Government and Employment Planning," in Proceedings of the National Conference of Social Work (New York: Columbia University Press, 1939), pp. 189-90.

54. FWA, *Report on the WPA Program*, 30 June 1941, pp. 46, 63, 84-87, 132.

55. FWA, *Final Report on the WPA*, pp. 67-68, 87, 90-92; and NA, RG 69, WPA Series 11, #045: Defense Training Programs, 1940-1943; #210.31: Mobilization of Women, 1941-1942; and #220.1: National Defense Projects, 1940-1942.

56. This preferential treatment was accorded only to veterans who had actually served, along with their widows and wives, as opposed to "peacetime veterans" who had been discharged from the military without seeing active duty. See FWA, *Final Report on the WPA*, p. 21; and Howard, *The WPA*, pp. 325-29.

57. Howard, *The WPA*, p. 321. The original wording adopted in 1939 stated that WPA funds could not be paid to anyone who advocated, or belonged to organizations that advocated, the overthrow of the government. The

following year it was changed to specifically exclude Communists, as well as members of Nazi Bund organizations. See FWA, *Final Report on the WPA*, p. 17; and Howard, *The WPA*, pp. 303-24.

58. Howard, *The WPA*, pp. 320-22.
59. Ibid., pp. 294-95.
60. Ibid., pp. 138-39, 294-95; and FWA, *Final Report on the WPA*, p. 63.

CONCLUSION

1. National Resources Planning Board, *National Resources Development Report for 1943. Part I: Post-War Plan and Program* (GPO, January 1943), pp. 3, 17; emphasis theirs. See also National Resources Planning Board, *Security, Work, and Relief Policies* (GPO, 1942).
2. Some of the programs designed to alter behaviors include: "learnfare," which docks payments for teenage parents if they have more than a certain number of unexcused absences from school; family caps, which do not increase checks for additional children conceived while a woman is receiving welfare; and "wedfare," which discounts a greater percentage of income in the computation of welfare payments.
3. Casey McKeever, *Memorandum about Governor Wilson's Proposed Budget Cuts* (Sacramento, CA: Western Center on Law and Poverty, 15 January 1992).

NOTES FOR TABLES AND FIGURES

Table 1: U.S. Bureau of the Census, *Historical Statistics of the United States, Colonial Times to 1970*, p. 126.
Figure 1: Works Projects Administration, *Final Statistical Report of the Federal Emergency Relief Administration* (Washington, DC: U.S. Government Printing Office, 1942), p. 46.
Figure 2: sames as Figure 1.
Figure 3: same as Table 1.
Figure 4: Figures from FWA, *Final Report of the WPA Program*, Table 8, "Average Number of Persons Employed on WPA Projects, by Program, August 1935-June 1943," p. 28.
Figure 5: Figures from ibid., Table 24, "Number of Women Employed on Projects Operated by WPA, December 1935-December 1942," p. 44.

INDEX